Grimsby Ontario Book 1 in Colour Photos, Saving Our History One Photo at a Time

Photography
by Barbara Raué
2017

Series Name:
Cruising Ontario

Book 185: Grimsby Book 1

Cover photo: 130 Main Street East, Page 15

Series Name: Cruising Ontario
Saving Our History One Photo at a Time
in colour photos

Books Available in Alphabetical Order:
Aberfoyle, Acton, Alton, Amherstburg, Ancaster, Arthur, Aylmer, Ayr, Bloomingdale, Brantford, Burlington, Caledon, Caledonia, Cambridge, Clifford, Conestogo, Delhi, Dorchester to Aylmer, Drayton, Drumbo, Dundas, Eden Mills, Elmira, Elora, Essex, Fergus, Guelph, Hagersville, Hamilton, Hanover, Harriston, Hespeler, Jarvis, Kingston, Kingsville, Kitchener, Linwood, Listowel, London, Lucknow, Mono, Mount Forest, Neustadt, New Hamburg, Niagara-on-the-Lake, Oakville, Orangeville, Orillia, Owen Sound, Palmerston, Peterborough, Petrolia, Port Elgin, Preston, Rockwood, Sarnia, Seaforth, Sheffield, Shelburne, Simcoe, Southampton, St. Jacobs, St. Marys, St. Thomas, Stoney Creek, Stratford, Thamesford, Tillsonburg, Waterdown, Waterford, Waterloo, Welland, Wellesley, Windsor, Wingham, Woodstock

Book 157: Brockville
Book 158: Merrickville
Book 159: Smiths Falls
Book 160: Portland, Newboro
Book 161: Westport & Area
Book 162: Perth
Book 163-166: Belleville ::
Book 167-168: Port Colborne
Book 169: Erin in Colour
Book 170: Goderich in Colour
Book 171: Sault Ste. Marie
Book 172: Lake Superior
Book 173-176: Thunder Bay
Book 177-179: Paris

Book 180-181: St. George
Book 182-183: Burford
Book 184: Mount Pleasant, Onondaga, Middleport
Book 185-186: Grimsby

Other Books by Barbara Raue

Coins of Gold

Arrows, Indians and Love

The Life and Times of Barbara

The Cromwell Family Book

Laura Secord Discovered

Daddy Where Are You?

Montana Series
Book 1: Montana Dream
Book 2: Life on the Montana Frontier
Book 3: Montana to Boston and Back
Book 4: Montana Sons Go to War
Book 5: Montana Sons Return From War

Visit Barbara's website to view all of her books
http://barbararaue.ca

Table of Contents

Main Street East   Page 7

Main Street West   Page 27

Architectural Terms   Page 61

Building Styles   Page 65

Grimsby is a town on Lake Ontario in the Niagara Region. It is named after the English fishing town of Grimsby in North East Lincolnshire. The majority of residents reside in the area bounded by Lake Ontario and the Niagara Escarpment. Grimsby has experienced significant growth over the past decade as the midpoint between Hamilton and St. Catharines.

The town of Grimsby was founded in 1790 (originally named Township Number 6 and then 'The Forty'), after a group of United Empire Loyalists settled at the mouth of 40 Mile Creek in 1787. A Loyalist from the Mohawk Valley, New York, Robert Nelles and his father and brothers were among the first to settle at The Forty following the American Revolution. Robert Nelles was a politician and later lieutenant-colonel in the War of 1812. In 1816 the village became known as Grimsby, the name of the surrounding township.

The town has gone through many changes, from being a small rural village; to a centre for the manufacture of farm machinery, hospital furniture, furnaces and other metal products; and later the hub of the Niagara Peninsula's fruit-growing industry. Grimsby had a successful fishing industry which lasted until the 1960s. The Town of Grimsby and the Township of North Grimsby were amalgamated in 1970 with the formation of the Regional Municipality of Niagara. With a number of wineries and distilleries, Grimsby now serves as the starting point for touring the Niagara wine region.

Grimsby is the birthplace of Hollywood director, Del Lord who rose to acclaim as the director of most of the Three Stooges short vaudeville comedies. Later, under Columbia Pictures, he directed nearly two hundred feature films.

Grimsby Beach was once a major holiday resort. Grimsby Park started in 1846 as a park for the Hamilton district of the Methodist Church. In 1910, the park's new owner, Harry Wylie, modernized the park with carousels, a motion picture theatre, and a "Figure 8" roller coaster. Operations continued until 1949, with attractions gradually closing and developers buying land to build houses.

Bisecting the town is the Queen Elizabeth Way. It has three exchanges in the town, with Casablanca Boulevard in the west, a central exchange for three roads (Christie Street, Ontario Street, and Maple Avenue), and Bartlett Avenue in the east.

The Grimsby Railway Station, on the south side of the railroad tracks west of Ontario Street and south of Queen Elizabeth Way, is served by the Maple Leaf train jointly operated by Via Rail and Amtrak.

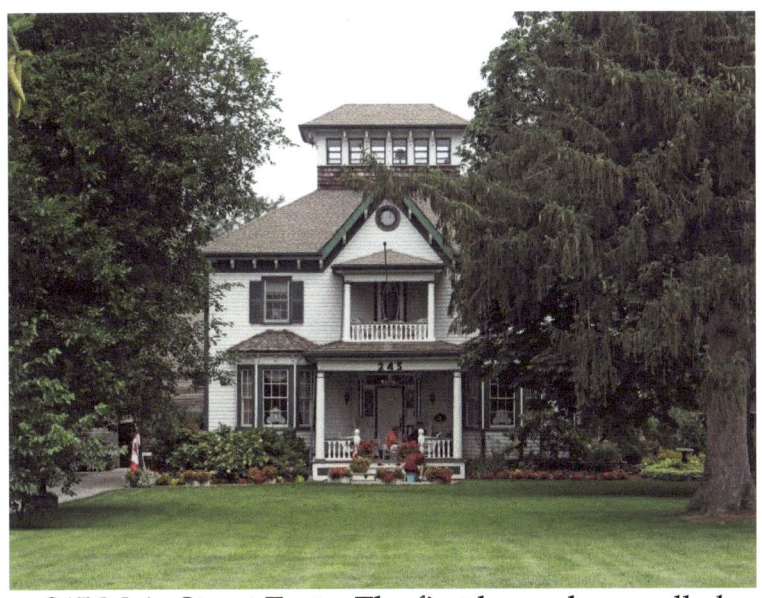

245 Main Street East – The first house here, called *Inchyra*, was built in 1846 by John Beamer Bowslaugh but was destroyed by fire in 1874 and was rebuilt as it is today. Bowslaugh was the benefactor of Grimsby Park.

The widow's walk was built around 1920. A widow's walk is a railed rooftop platform, originally designed to observe vessels at sea. The name comes from the wives of mariners who would watch for their spouses to return. In some instances, the ocean took the lives of the mariners, leaving the women as widows; they would often gaze out to sea wishing that their loved ones would return home and the name widow's walk was born.

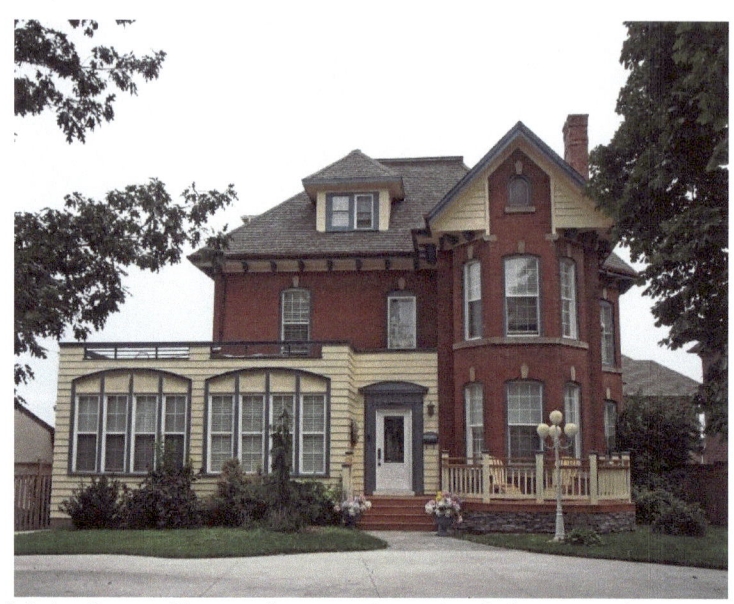

239 Main Street East – dormer in attic, 2½-storey bay window

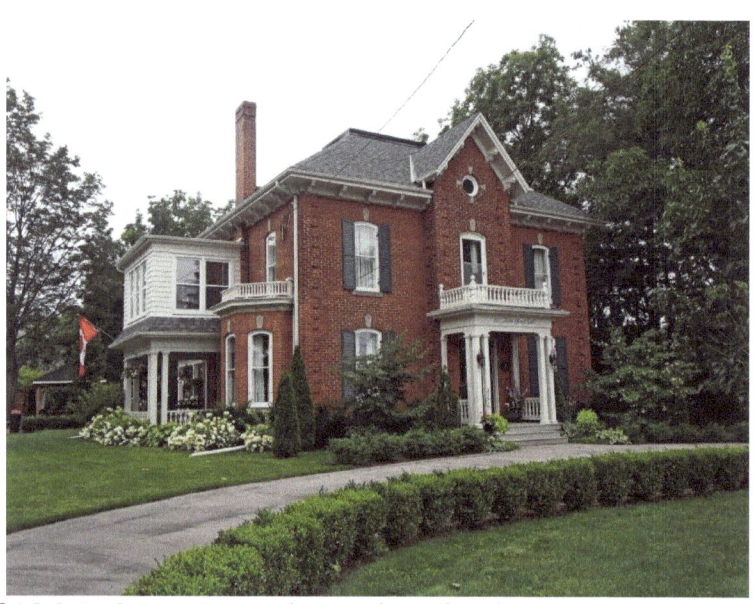

224 Main Street East – hipped roof, 2½-storey frontispiece, second floor balconies, bay window

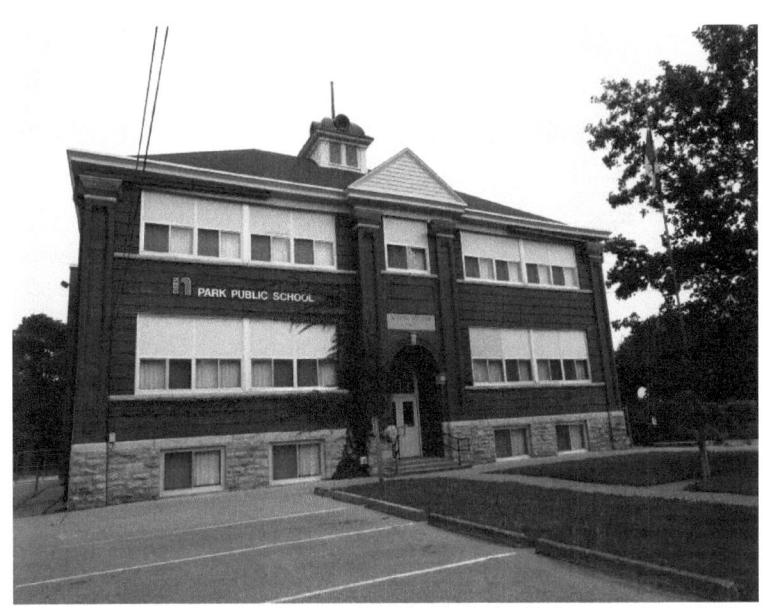

217 Main Street East – Park Public School - In 1805, School Section (S.S.) No. 1 North Grimsby Township was built of logs on what is now known as Park Road. A frame building was erected on the southeast corner of Park Road and what is now Regional Road 81 in1825. This building served as the school until 1865, when a one room red brick schoolhouse was built. The first teacher was Walter H. Nelles. In those early days, the teacher boarded with a nearby family. The teacher's board paid for the tuition for the children in the family. Fifty cents a week was paid to the family responsible for starting the fire in the school every morning, and another fifty cents went to those who swept and dusted the school.

By 1909, a larger school was needed because of the growing number of people living in the Grimsby Beach area to the north of the school. A four-room brick building was constructed on the present site on a two acre parcel of land. As the school board had decided in 1909 to build the school much larger than needed, it wasn't until 1951 that expansion was necessary. Two classrooms were added, and modern flush toilets and heating were installed.

Further expansion took place in 1954, with the addition of two classrooms, a principal's office, a staff room and the conversion of two storage rooms into classrooms, bringing the school to its present size. At the same time, a further 2/3 acre of land was added. In the 1990's the property to the west of the school was acquired. Park School has operated at capacity since the last expansion and now uses one portable classroom as well.

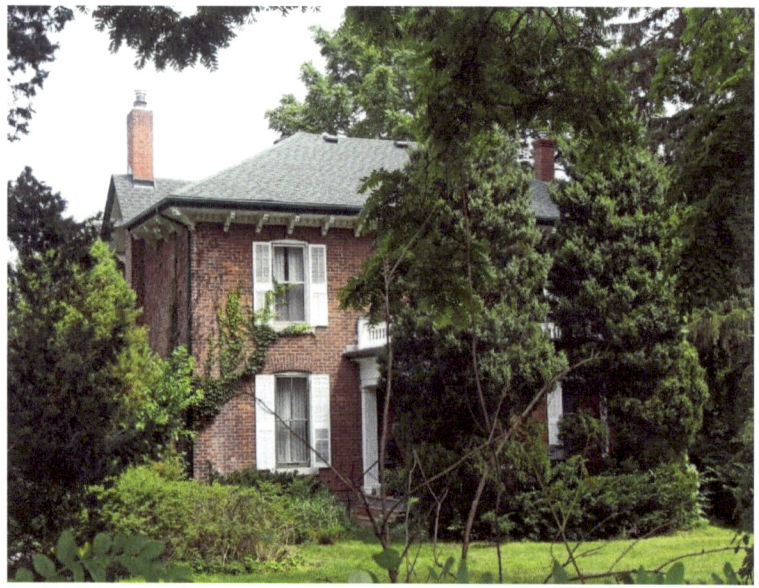

203 Main Street East - The Denwycke House was built in the 1840s in the Georgian style with Neo-Classical features such as the front porch, upstairs veranda and deep bracketed eaves. Georgian architecture is characterized by proportion and balance. It was originally the home of Peter Van Duser.

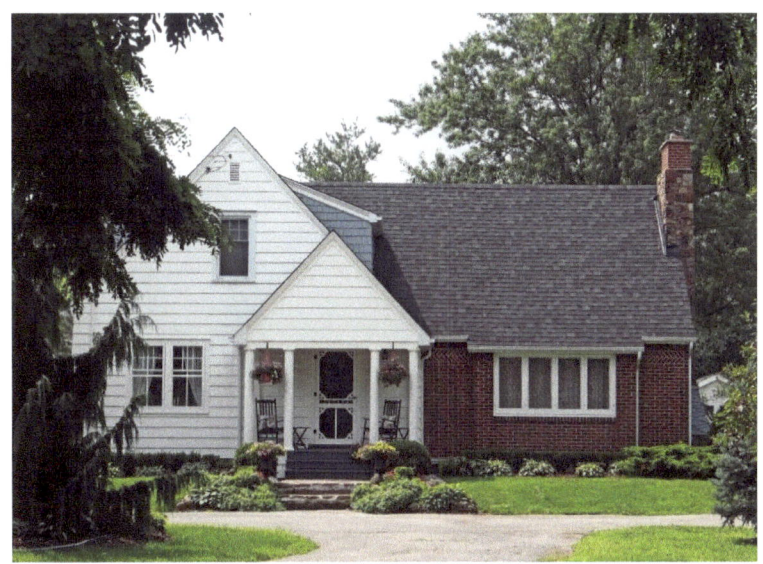

174 Main Street East - Vernacular

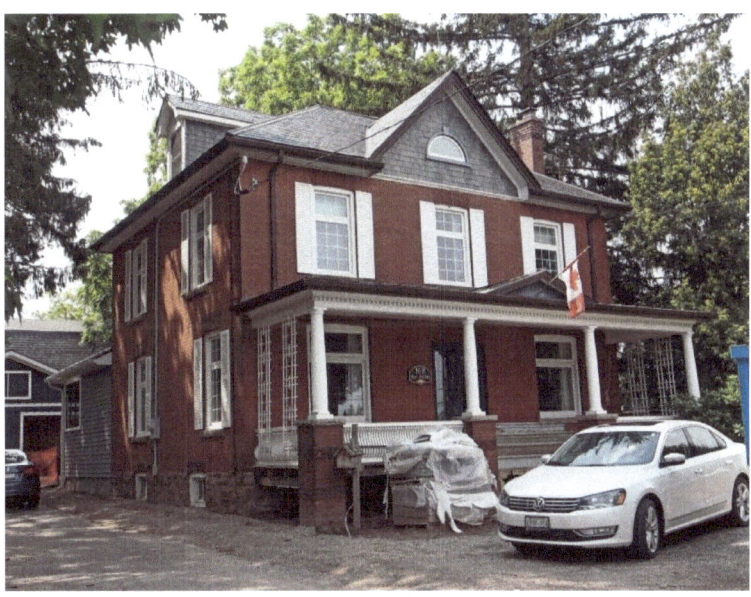

168 Main Street East - dormer

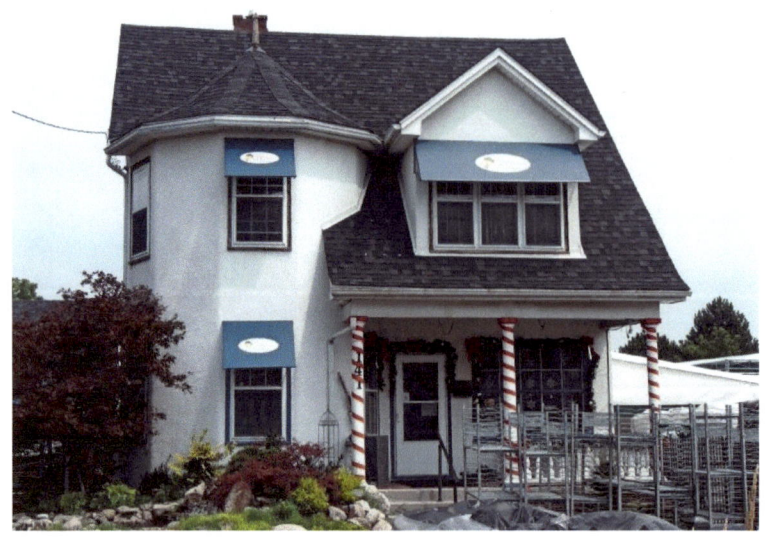

141 Main Street East – Cole's Christmas Cottage Gift Shop

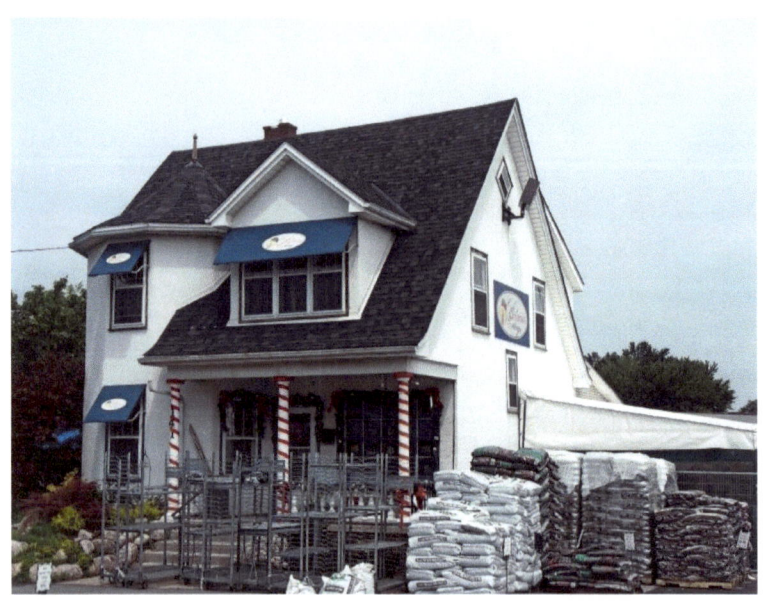

141 Main Street East

In 1891 Albert Edward Cole erected a 1,000 square foot greenhouse on the former sawmill property in Grimsby, and grew violets and vegetables. A.E. Cole's three sons were involved at an early age selling vegetables and delivering flowers. By 1930 the greenhouse was expanded to 25,000 square feet. Cole's three sons, John, Gordon and Norman, purchased the business in 1932 and more expansion followed as the floral industry grew. The children and grandchildren all worked to make Cole's a success! In 1957 Norman Cole & Elizabeth became sole owners of the business and they ran the business together for 29 years. After 95 years of family ownership, Cole's Florist was sold to Harry DeVries in 1986.

Harry and Nancy DeVries opened West Lincoln Florist in Smithville in 1982. While making a delivery in February 1986, Harry expressed interest in purchasing Cole's and the sale took place on October 4, 1986. Ten days after, the business was moved across the street when Harry purchased the property from the Cole family. The old blue house was carefully converted to a 1,200 square foot store. By February of 1987 the small cottage next to the store was torn down to construct a 3,000 square foot greenhouse. An additional 1,200 square feet were added for more storage and deliveries. In 1995 the Garden Centre expanded with the addition of another Greenhouse in the centre of the yard to house many hanging plants and annuals.

In 2006 Cole's Garden Décor was opened across the street. In 2011 Cole's expanded its water garden department moving it to the location of the Garden Décor store. Cole's Pond Store is a one stop shop for water garden enthusiasts.

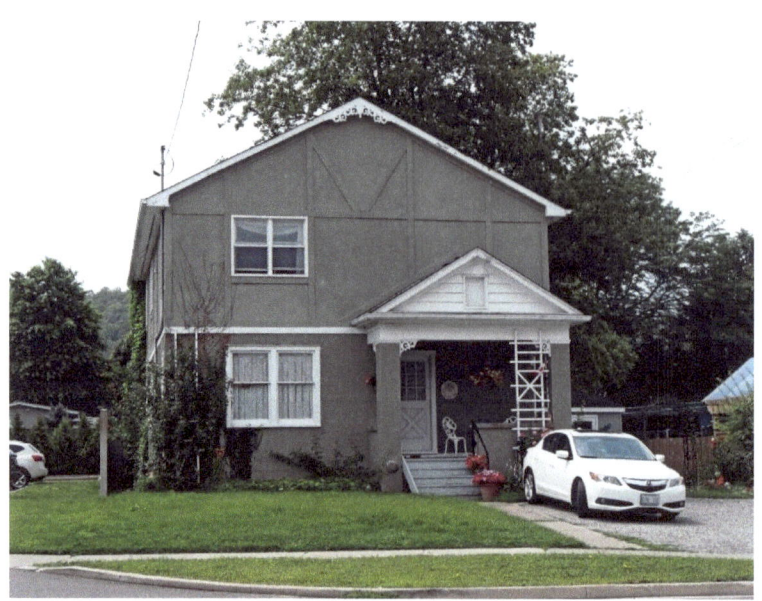
140 Main Street East

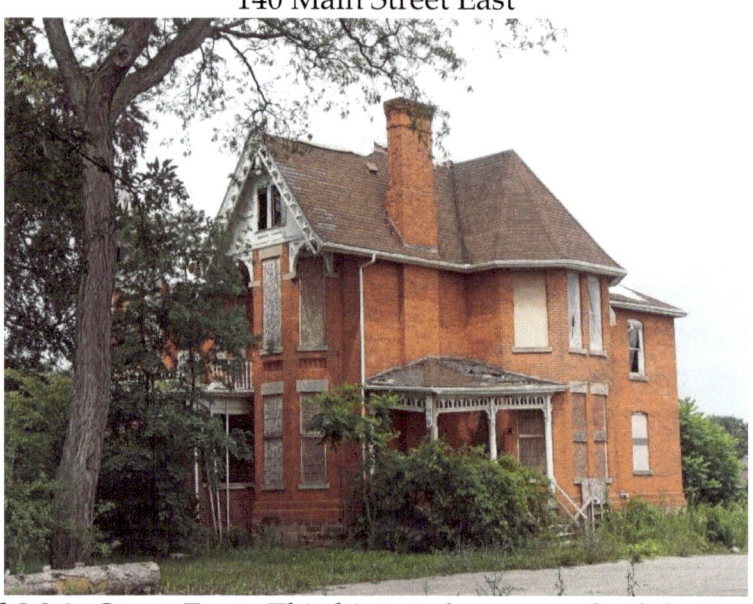
133 Main Street East - This historic home was built by James William Grout Nelles circa 1865, and later became the home of his son Willison Boise Nelles and his wife Henrietta.

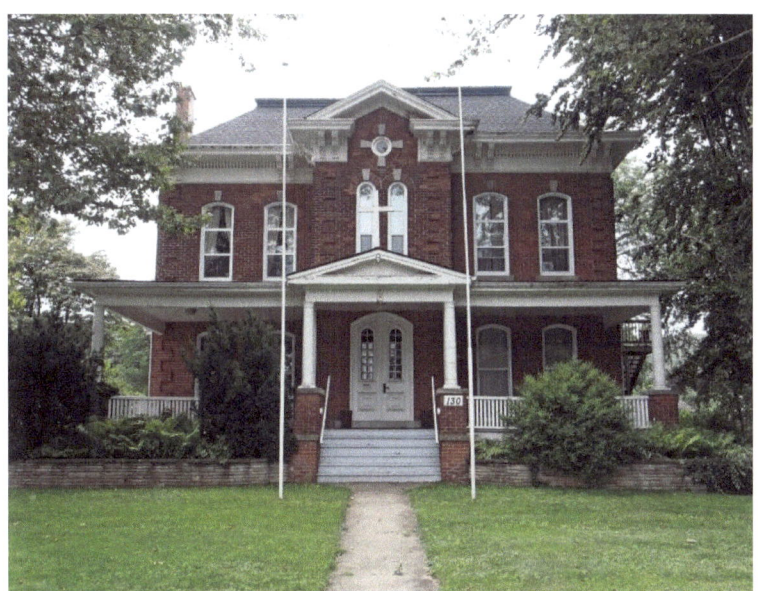

130 Main Street East – Walter Nelles, son of Peter Ball Nelles and his wife Mary Sumner, built this Italianate style house with a hipped roof with deck, 2½-storey frontispiece, paired cornice brackets, voussoirs and keystones, corner quoins, pediment above entrance.

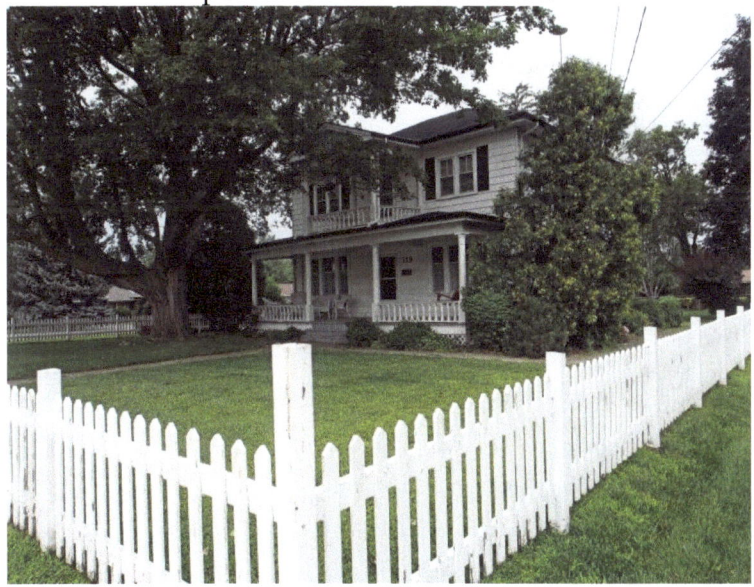

119 Main Street East – 2nd floor balcony, pediment

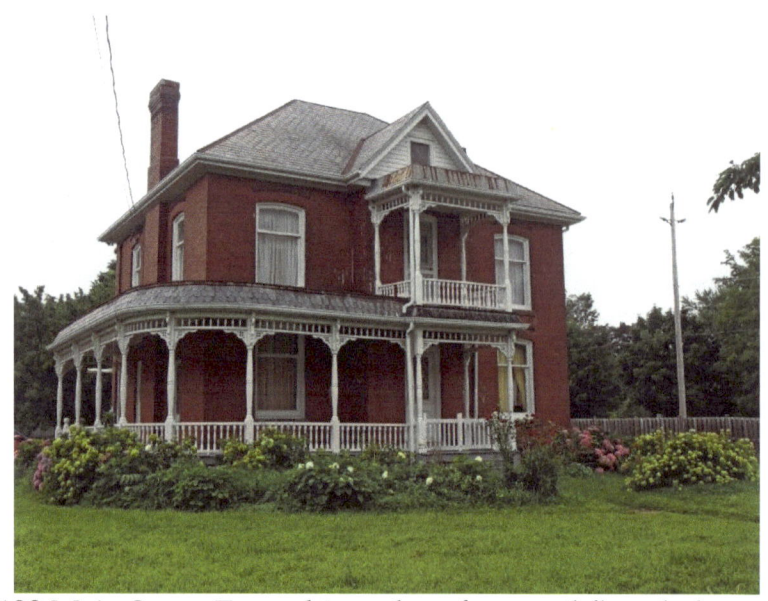

122 Main Street East – hipped roof, second floor balcony, wraparound veranda

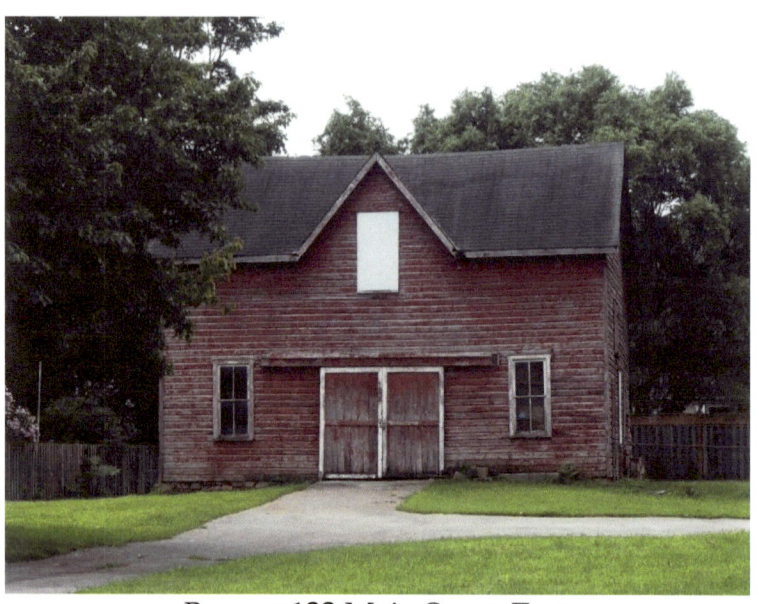

Barn at 122 Main Street East

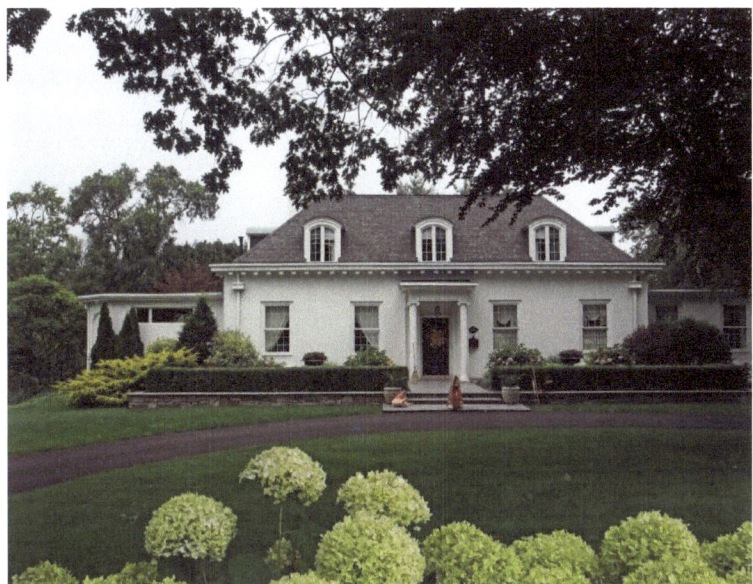

111 Main Street East – It has a French influence and was built in the 1920s by a Toronto lawyer as a summer home for his parents. There are dormers in the roof, and Ionic pillars surrounding entrance.

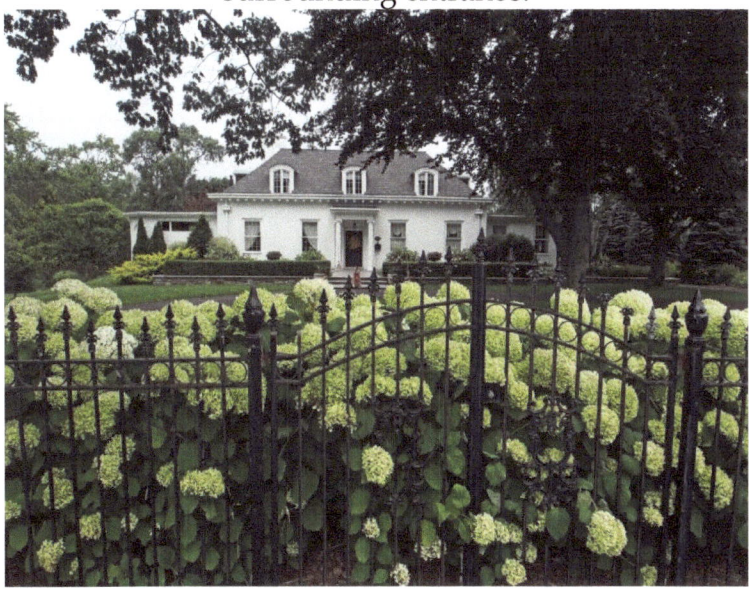

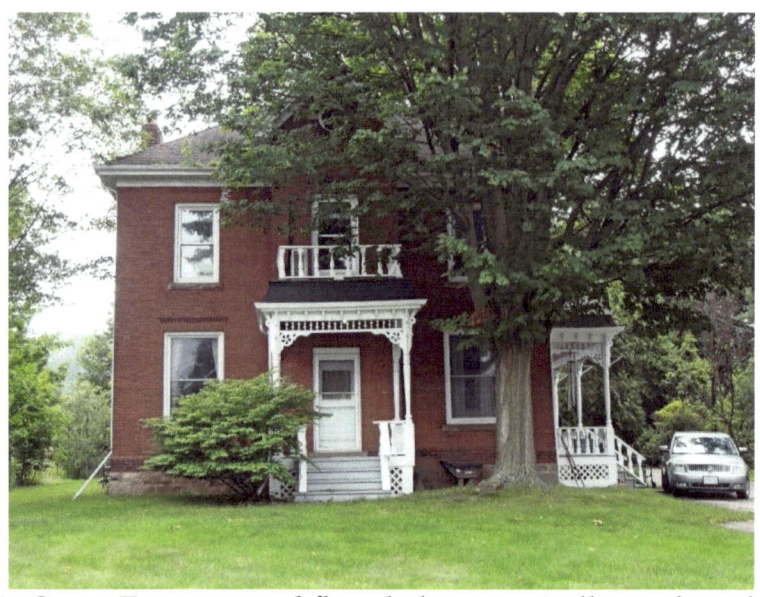

Main Street East – second floor balcony, spindle work on front and side porches

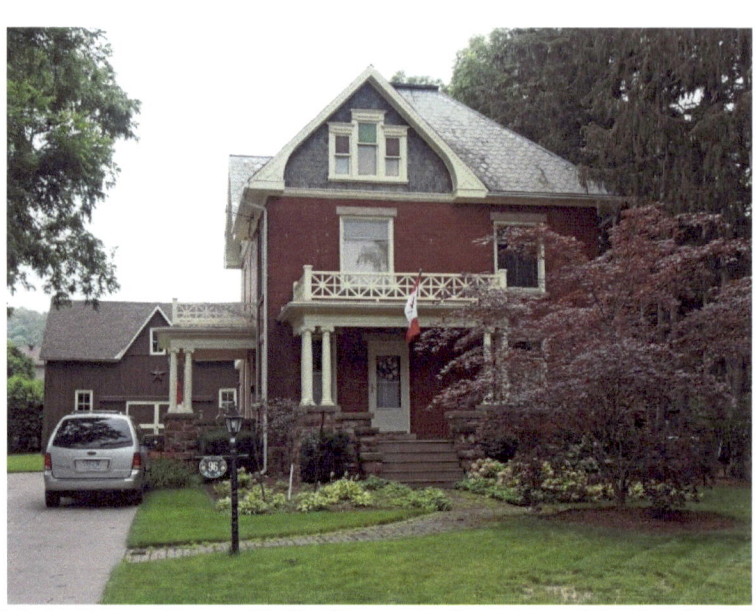

96 Main Street East – Palladian window in gable, Ionic pillars supporting front and side second floor balconies

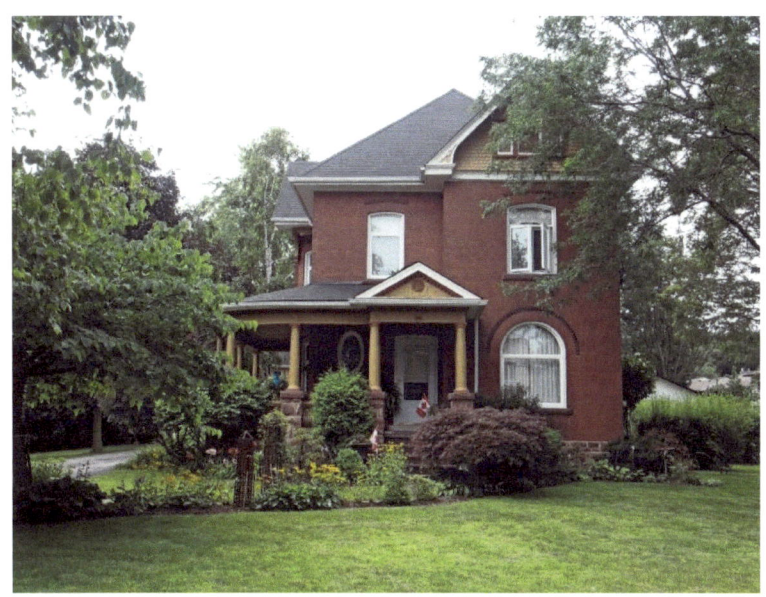

92 Main Street East – wraparound veranda with Doric pillars, pediment, voussoirs

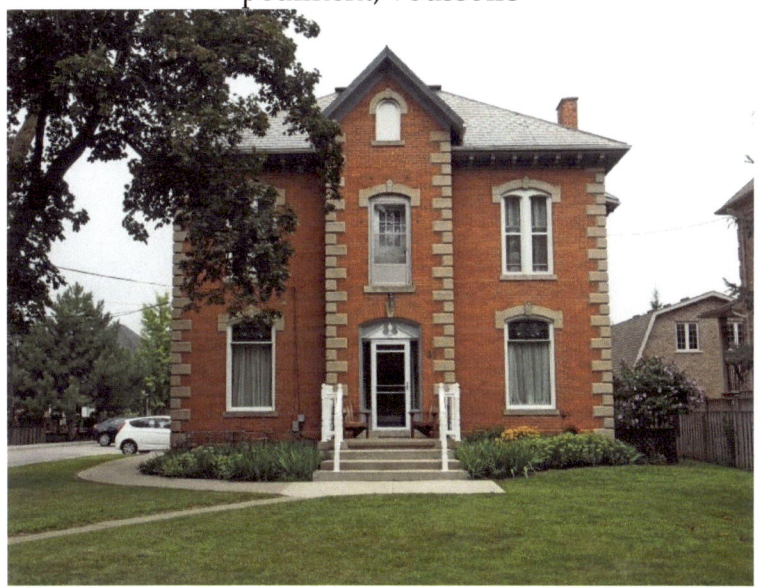

91 Main Street East – 2½-storey frontispiece, dichromatic corner quoining, cornice brackets, broken pediment above door

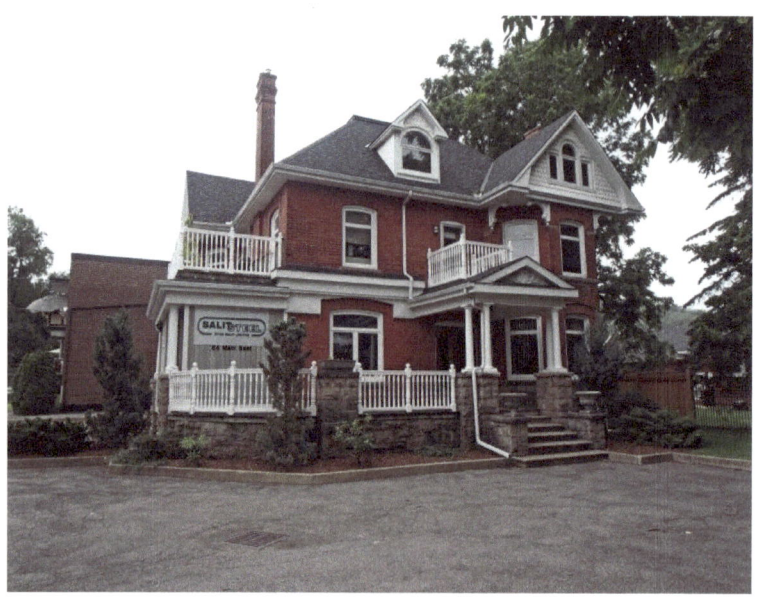

84 Main Street East – dormer in attic, Palladian window in gable, Doric pillars supporting porches with second floor balconies, pediment

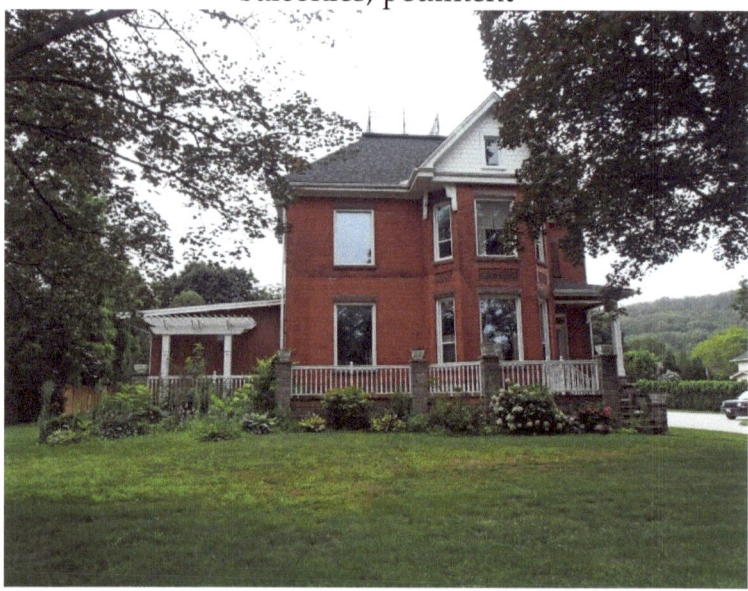

Main Street East – Faithshire Place circa 1880 - 2½-storey tower-like bay window, fretwork, widow's walk on roof

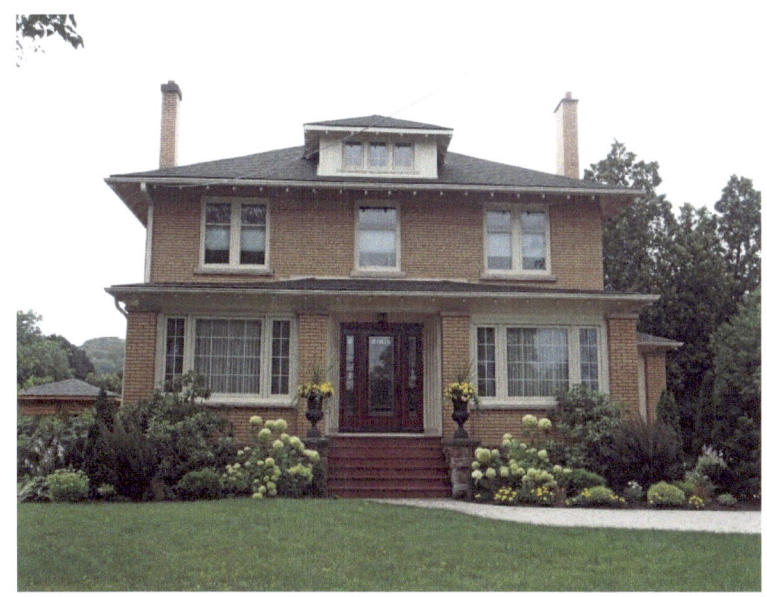

78 Main Street East – hipped roof with dormer, sidelights

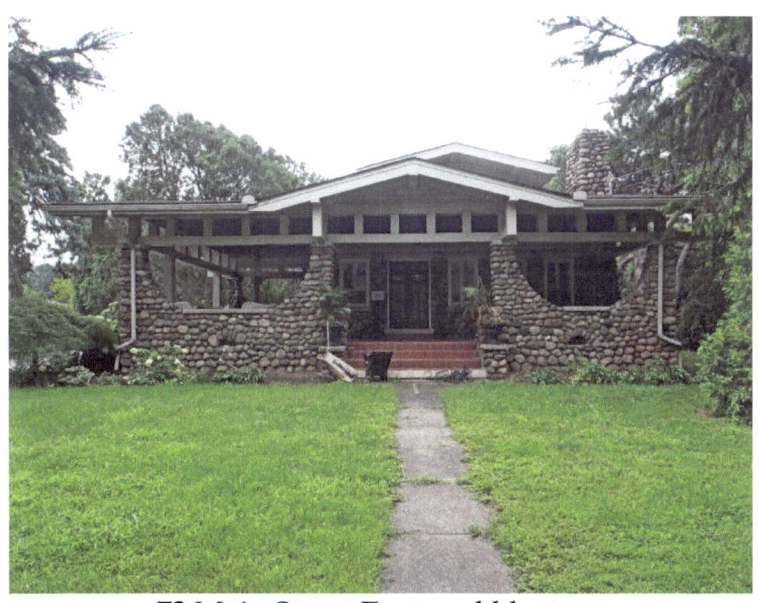

72 Main Street East - cobblestone

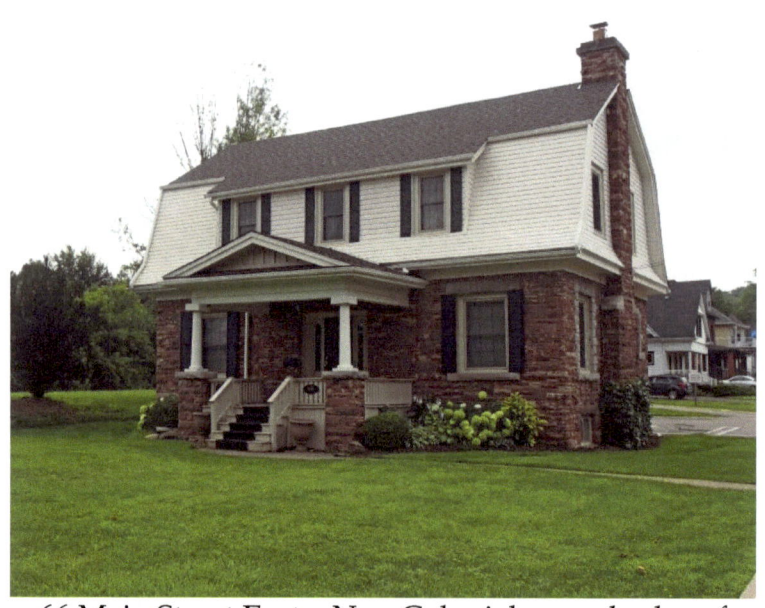

66 Main Street East – Neo-Colonial – gambrel roof

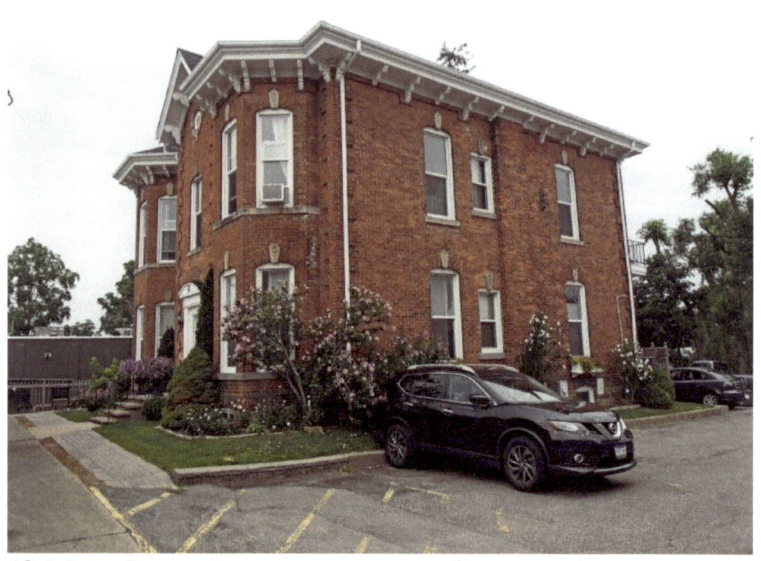

43 Main Street East – two-storey bay windows, cornice brackets

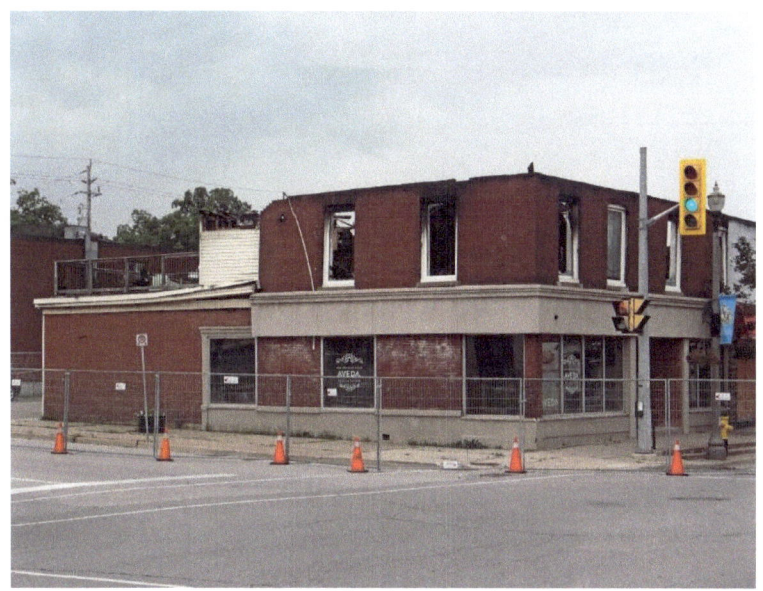

Remains of building after fire

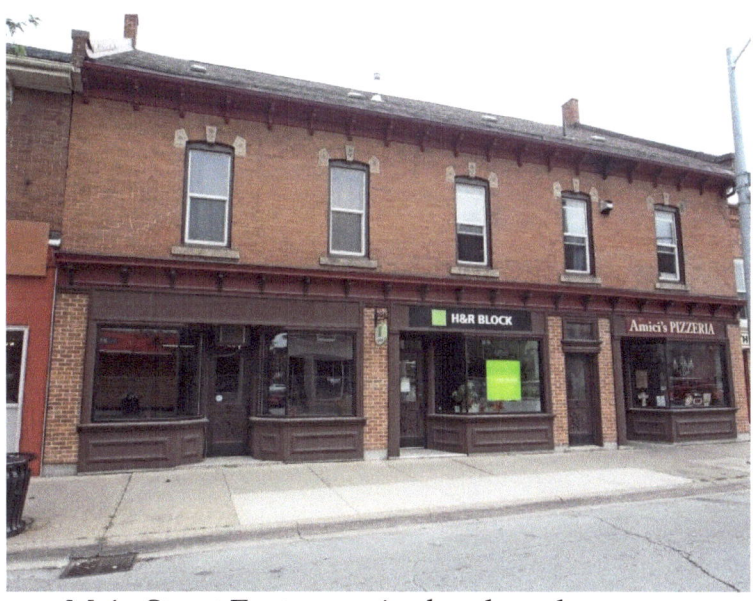

Main Street East – cornice brackets, keystones

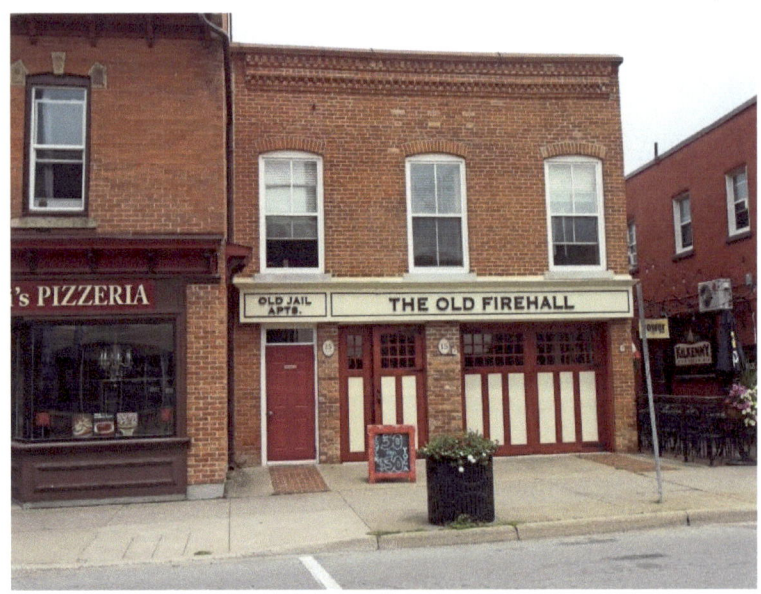

14 Main Street East – The Old Fire Hall – dentil molding

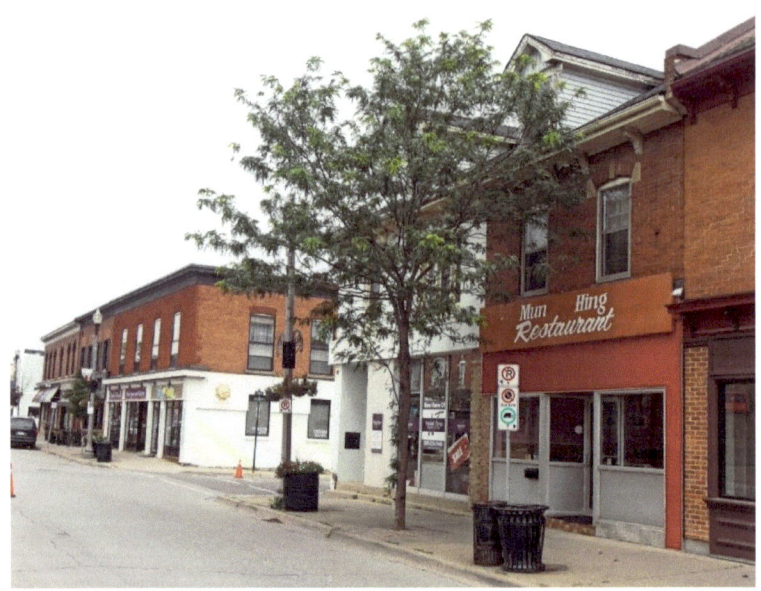

3 Main Street East – Mun Hing Restaurant. When the Hamilton, Grimsby & Beamsville Electric Railway was constructed in the 1890s, the tracks ran along this street.

The railway carried passengers and shipments of fruit between Beamsville and Hamilton until 1931.

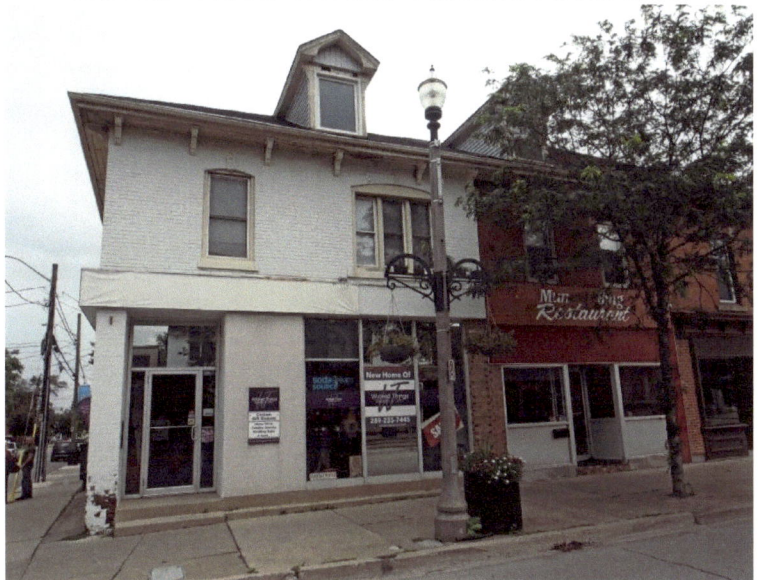

1 Main Street East - dormer

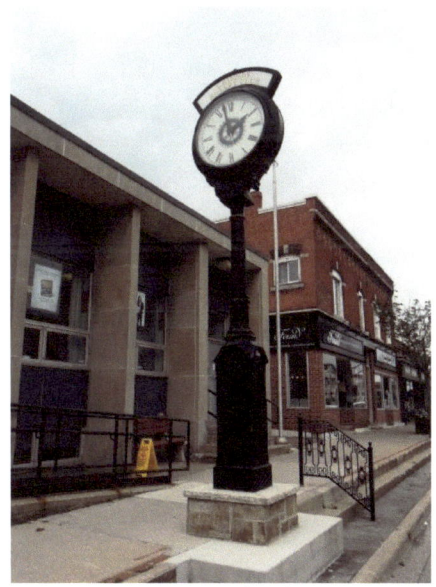

Town clock

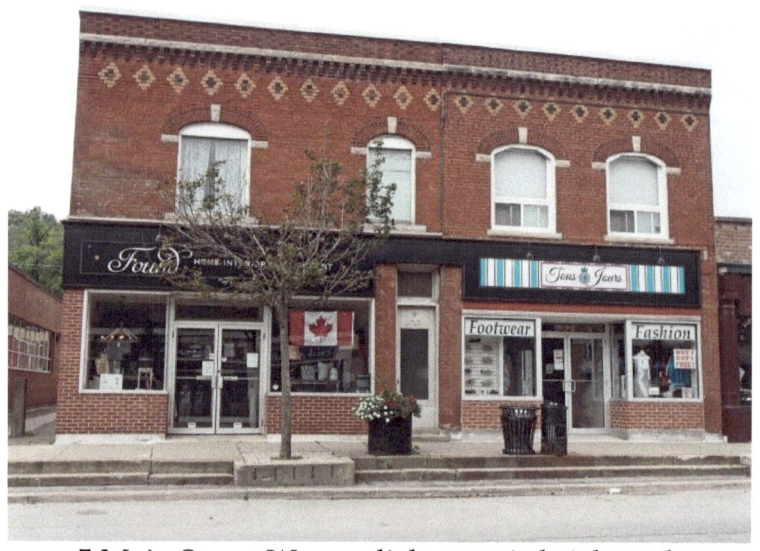

5 Main Street West – dichromatic brickwork

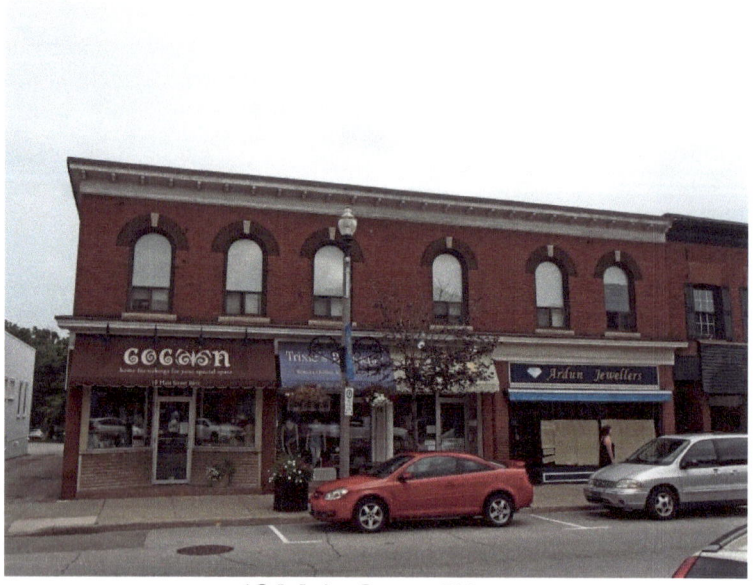

18 Main Street West

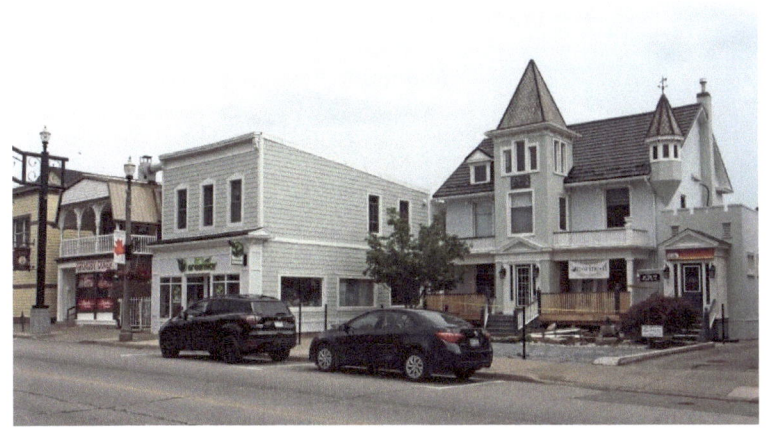

Main Street West

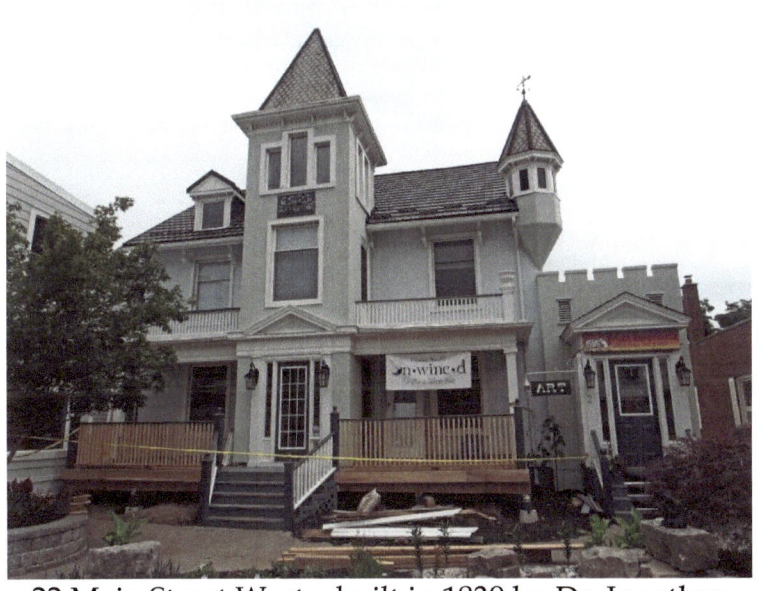

22 Main Street West – built in 1839 by Dr. Jonathan Woolverton. It was his home and office until his death in 1883. It has a three-storey tower, turret, dormer, second floor balconies, pediments above doors with sidelights, battlement above door to right of picture

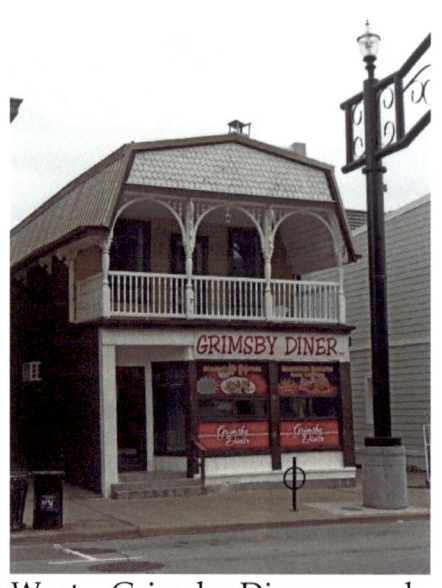

26 Main Street West – Grimsby Diner - gambrel roof, second floor balcony

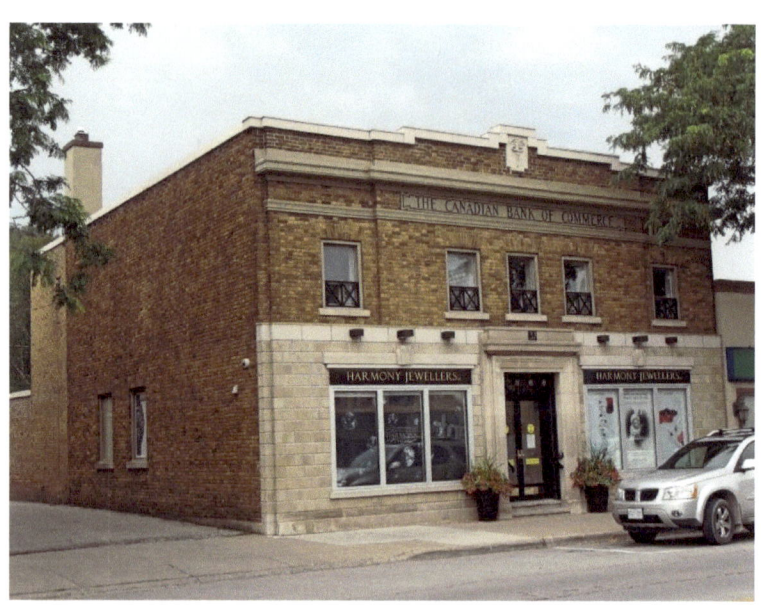

37 Main Street West – The Canadian Bank of Commerce building – now Harmony Jewellers - keystones

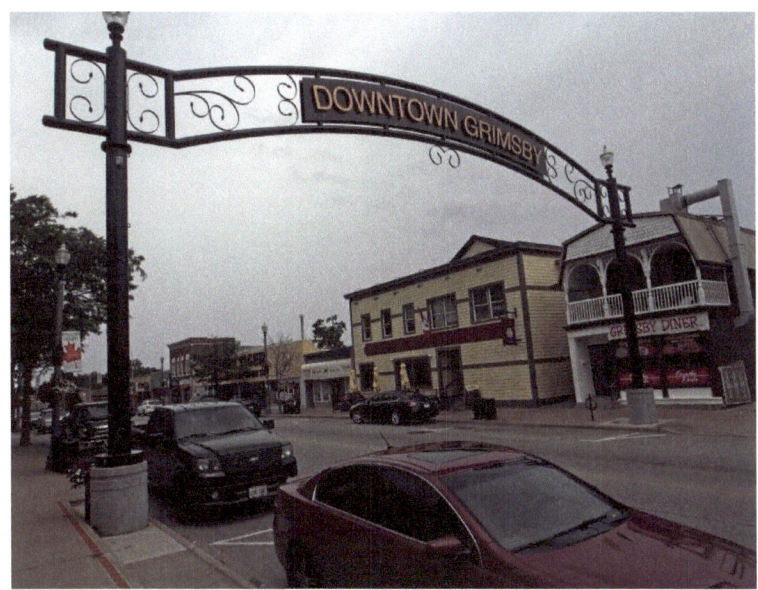

This main thoroughfare of Main Street East and West was originally called the Queenston Stone Road, as it extended all the way to Niagara. It included King Street in Stoney Creek, King Street in Beamsville, and St. Paul Street in St. Catharines. Later, it was known officially as Ontario Highway #8, then as Regional Road 81.

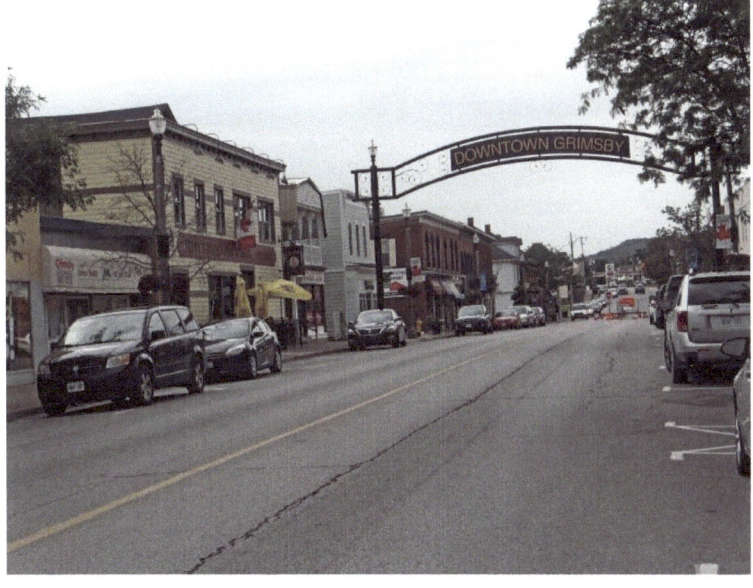

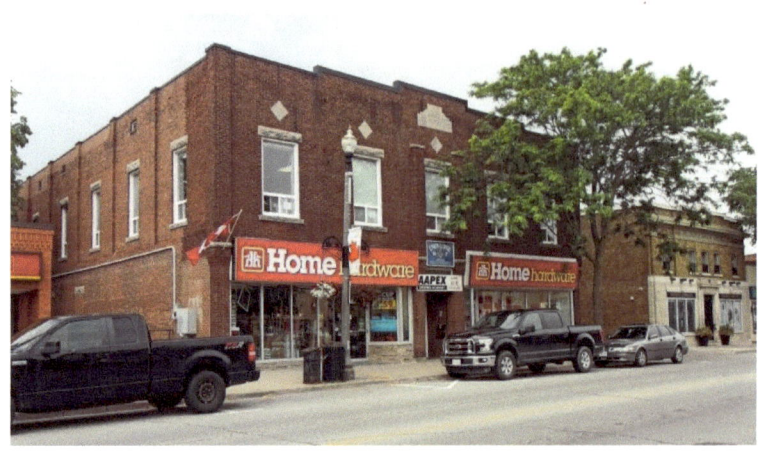

35 Main Street West

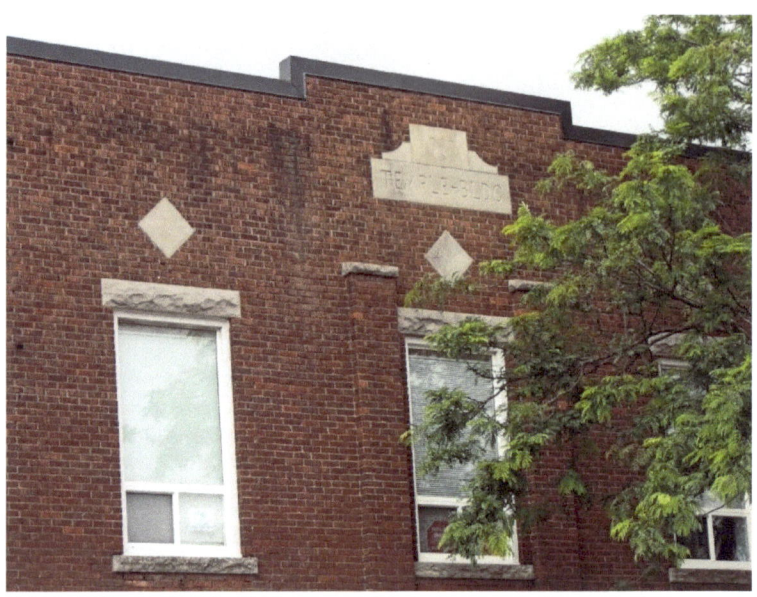

Temple Building – 1919 – stepped parapet

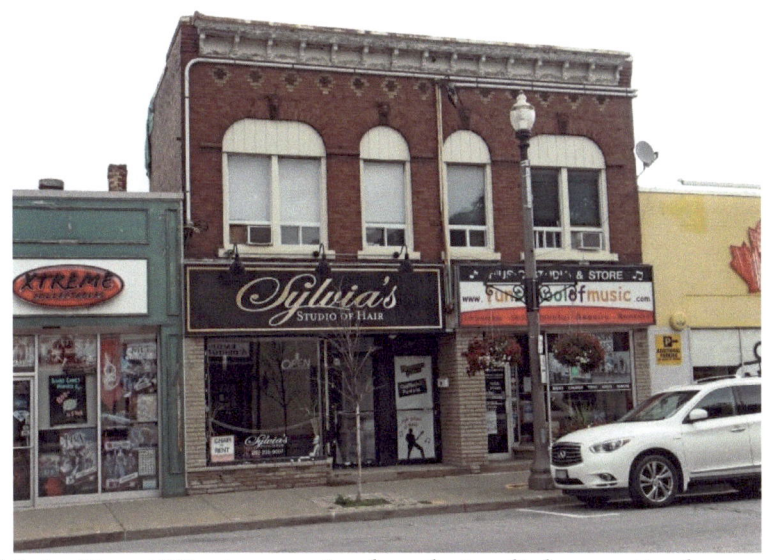

44 Main Street West – cornice brackets, dichromatic decorative brickwork

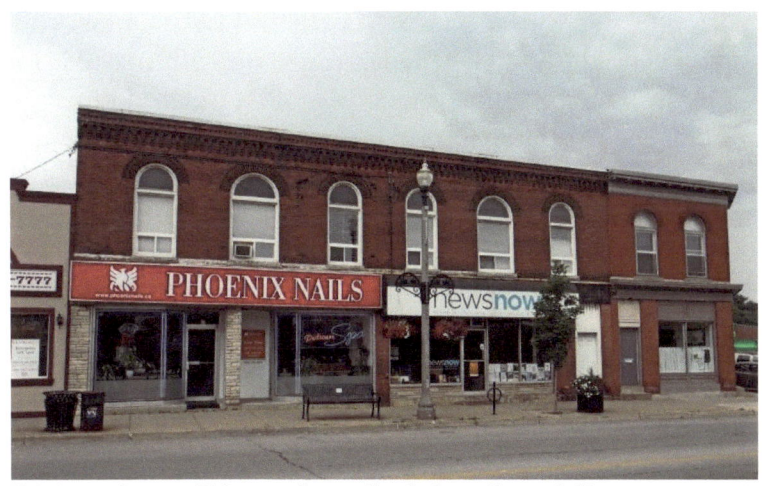

47 Main Street West – bevelled dentil molding, voussoirs above windows

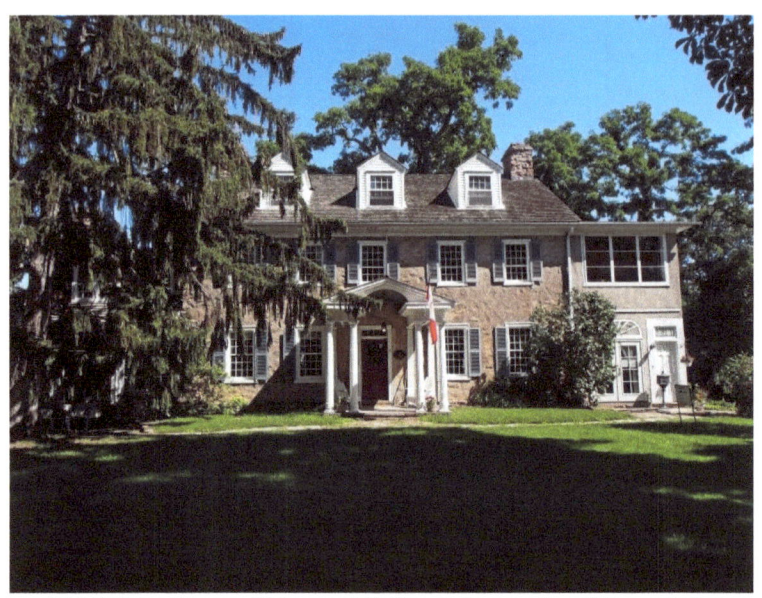

126 Main Street West – Nelles Manor is a historic home completed in 1798 by Colonel Robert Nelles, a Loyalist from the Mohawk Valley, New York. The house is considered to be the oldest inhabited dwelling between Niagara and Kingston. It was built in the Georgian style of locally quarried stone over a ten year period (1788-98). Built facing north and Lake Ontario on an old path called Squire Nelles' Lane, the main entrance was later moved to the south on the other side, with a pillared porch facing on to the new Stone Road (now Main Street). The Neo-Classical portico was added in the early 1820s.

This home served as Nelles' residence during his lengthy career as Justice of the Peace, Member of the Legislative Assembly and Commander of the 14th Lincoln Militia. Colonel Nelles' office was a small room on the north side, where he performed many marriages before clergy were available. The house was a centre for gala events and remained in the Nelles family possession until 1963. It has seven fireplaces, walnut woodwork and spacious halls and rooms. Originally a private residence, it was turned into a museum in 2016 and is now open to the public.

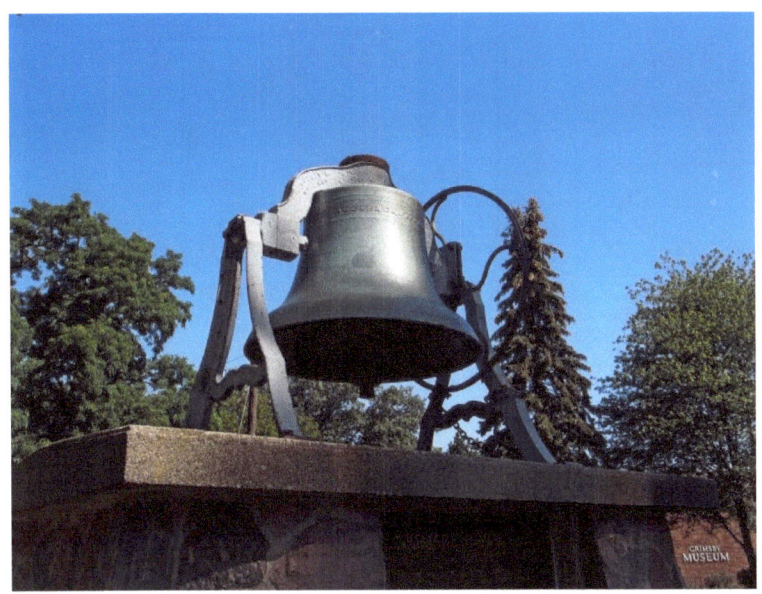

The town bell was purchased for the fire department in 1883 and placed on John Grout's foundry on the corner of Main and Oak Streets. For 75 years it summoned firemen, signified working hours, and proclaimed curfews. It pealed for celebrations, the ending of wars, and to honor championship hockey teams. It tolled out the old year and rang in the New Year. The bell was restored in 1966 and rang in the Centennial year and has rung in special occasions since then.

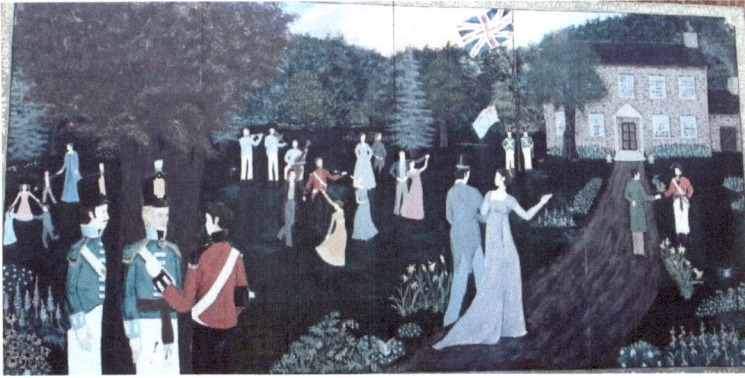

Mural

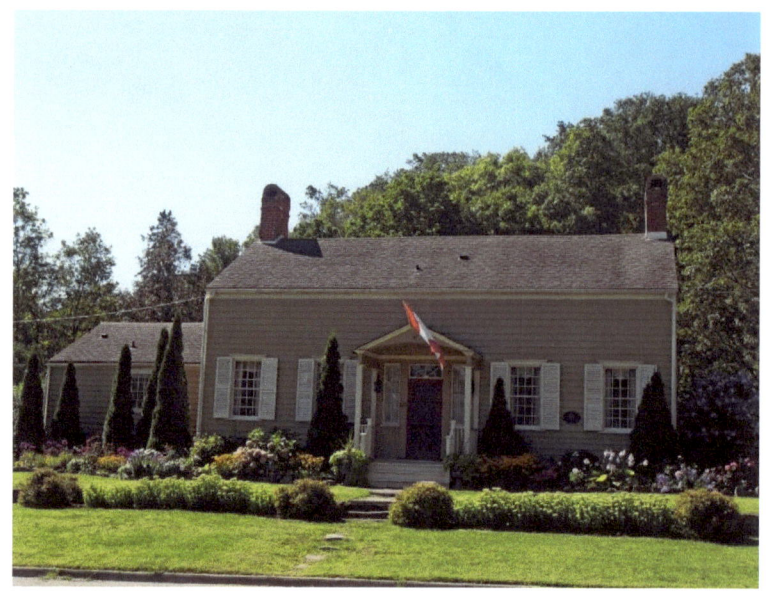

125 Main Street West – The south wing of this simple Georgian Colonial house is Robert Nelles' original log home built in 1787 as a temporary residence while the Manor across the road was constructed. It was used as a barracks during the War of 1812 and had a prison cell in the basement.

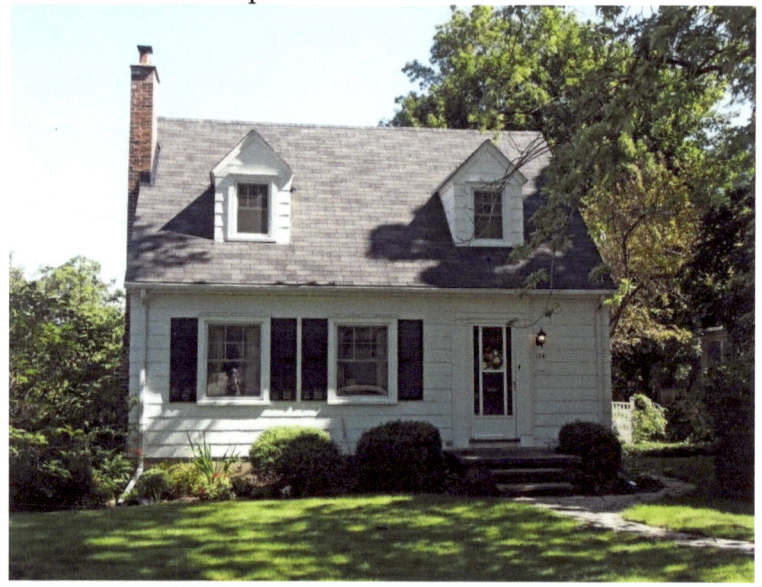

154 Main Street West - dormers

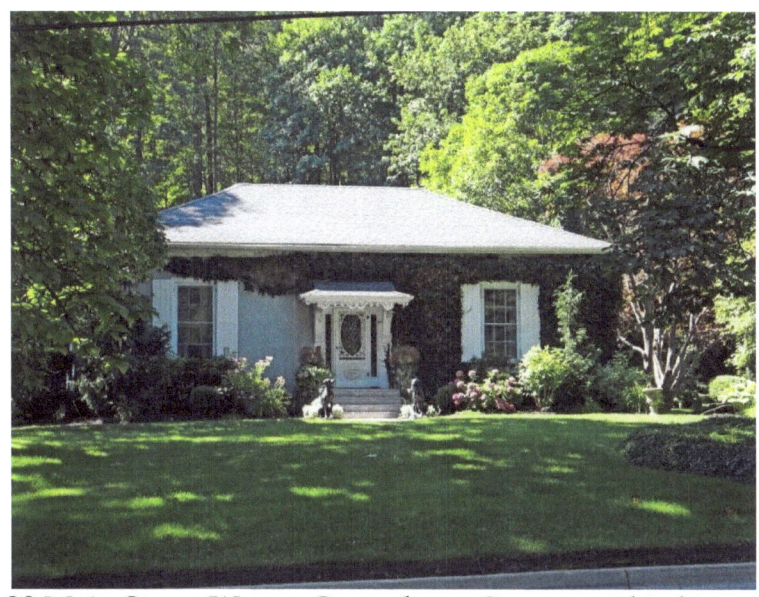

129 Main Street West – Canterbury Cottage - This historic home was built in 1852 by Charles Nelles, son of Robert, and was deeded to his widowed half-sister Catharine Bingle Porter. Catharine was the daughter of Robert Nelles' second wife, Maria Bingle. This Regency cottage with its low hip roof and large windows has a cozy appearance that hides its spacious, elegant interior. Two additions have been made to the rear of this home. The bent Catalpa tree in front of the house was once said to be a marker on an early Indian trail, leading south to flint beds in Wainfleet.

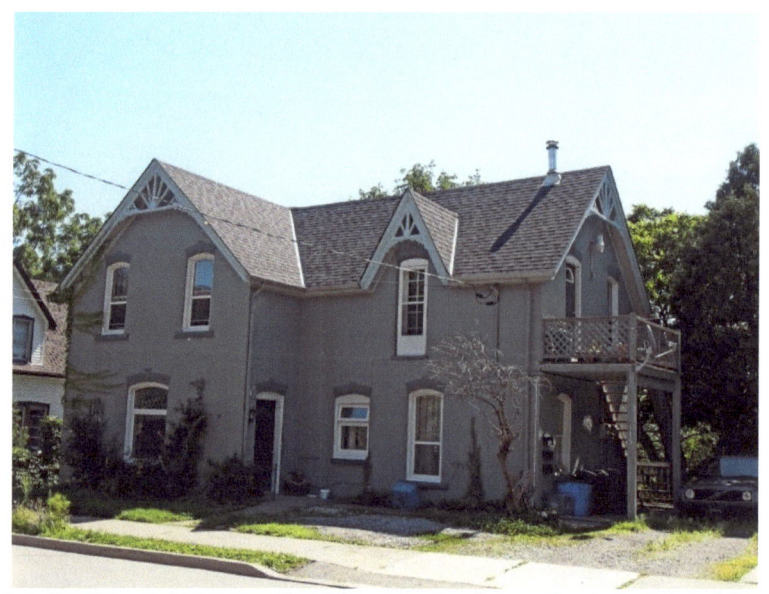

Main Street West – Gothic – verge board trim on gables

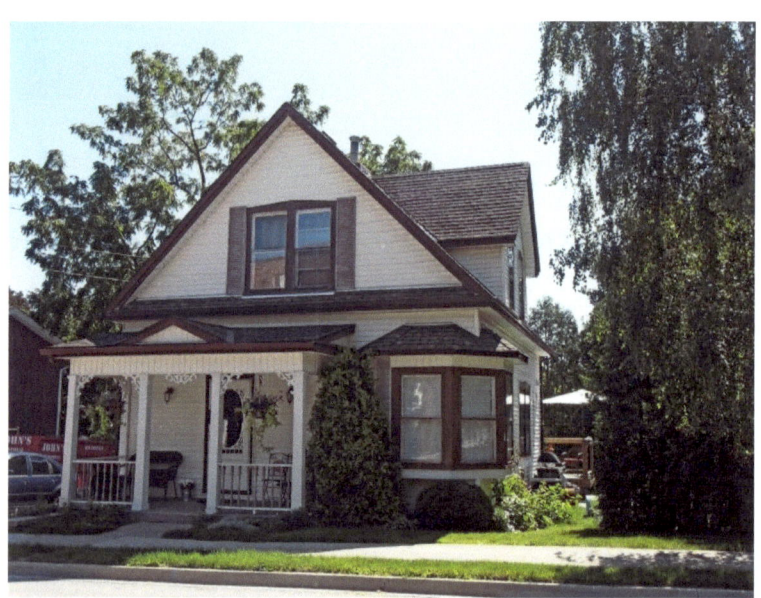

Main Street West – bay window

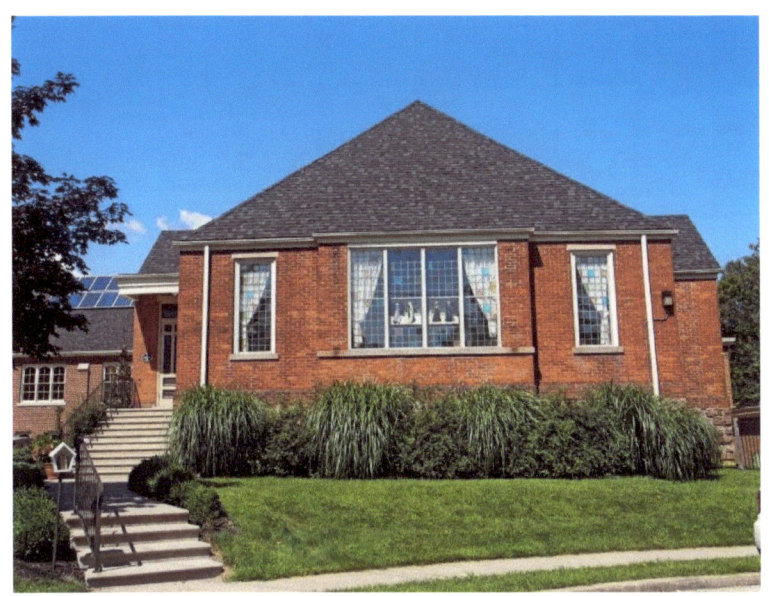

Older part
100 Main Street West – Trinity United Church

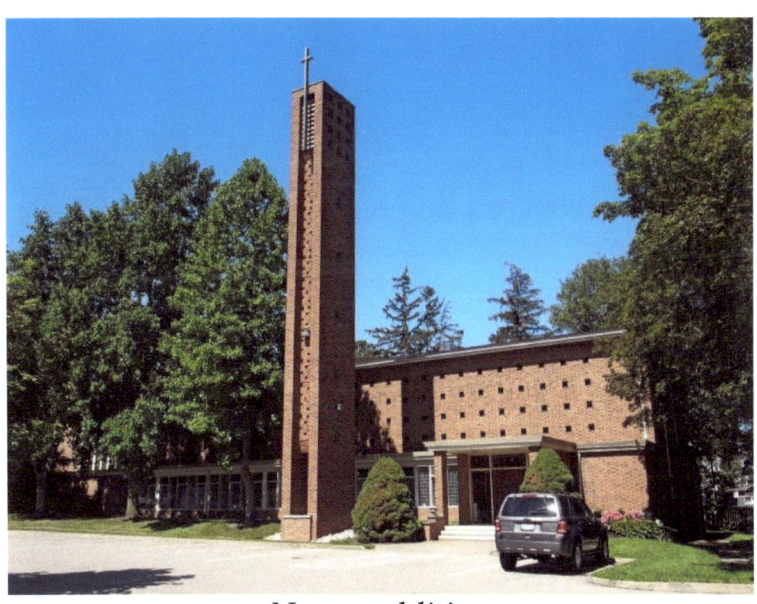

Newer addition

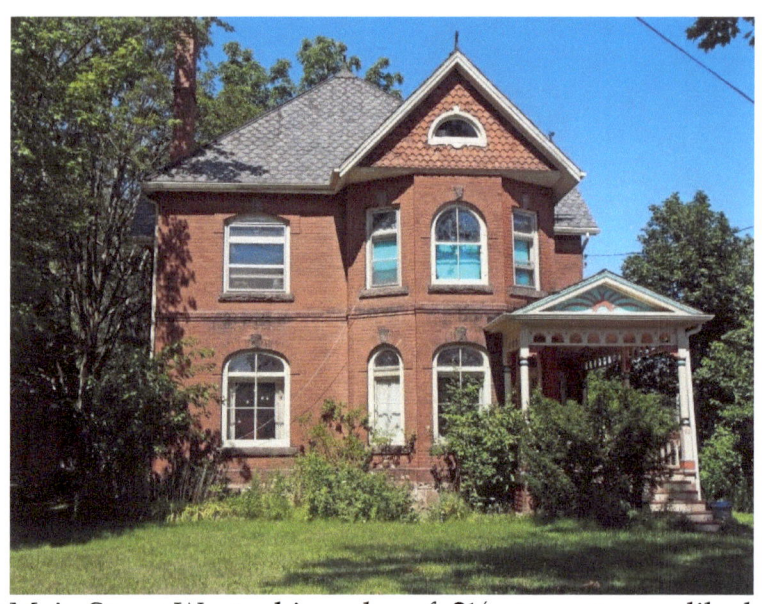

92 Main Street West – hipped roof, 2½-storey tower-like bay with half-circle window in gable, voussoirs and keystones, pediment above porch

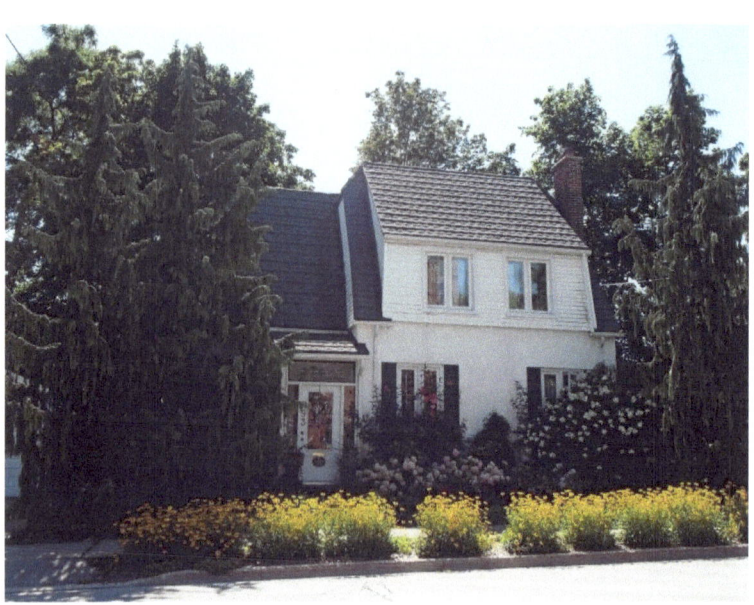

93 Main Street West – large dormer

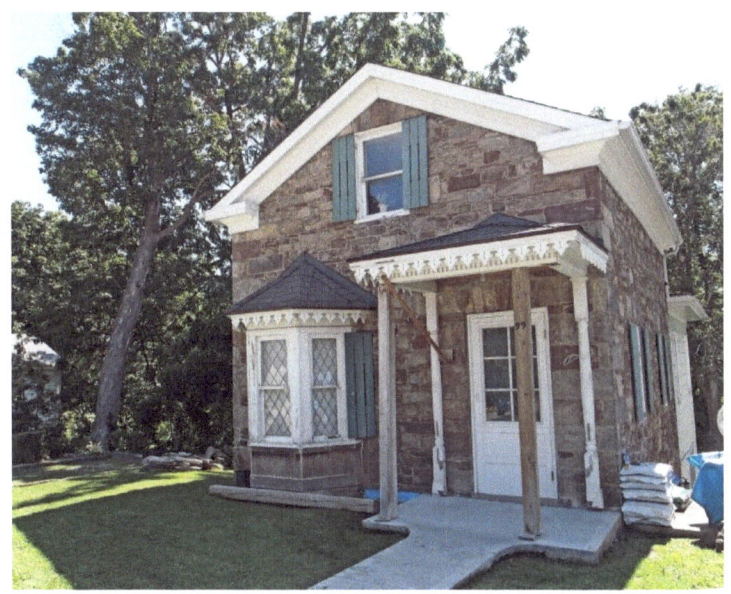

99 Main Street West - This small stone cottage is believed to have been built for the Nelles family seamstress by a stone mason who used the stone left over from the building of Nelles Manor. A resident seamstress was a necessity since manufactured garments were not available in pioneer Upper Canada. It is believed to date from about 1812.

Ann, the present owner, has lived there for twenty-seven years.

Gothic – cornice return on gable, bay window

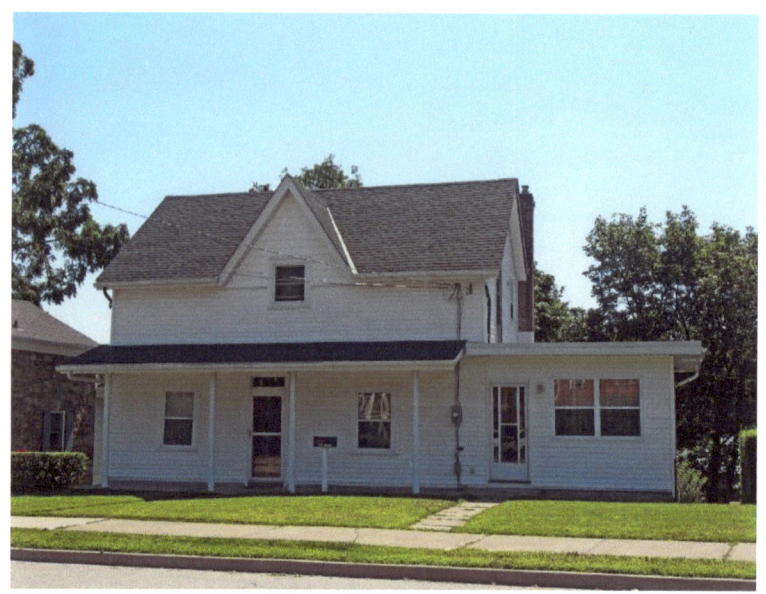
Main Street West

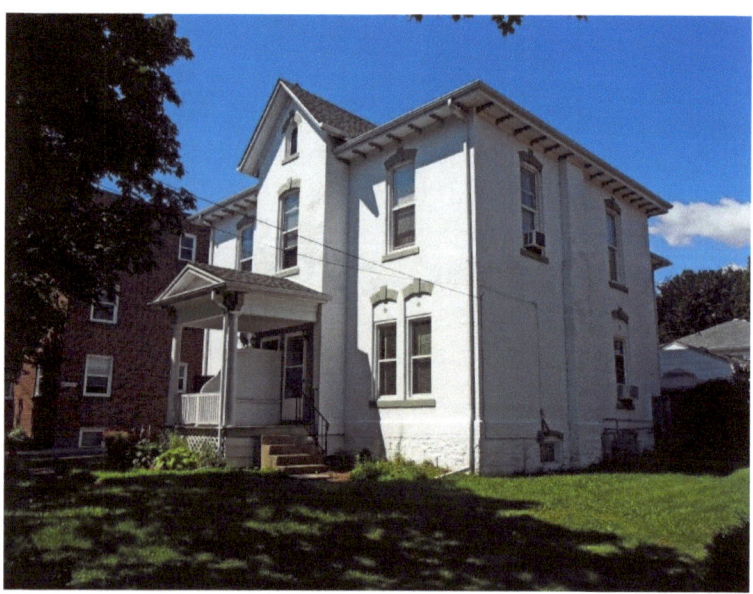
Main Street West – 2½-storey frontispiece, cornice brackets, voussoirs and keystones, pediment above porch

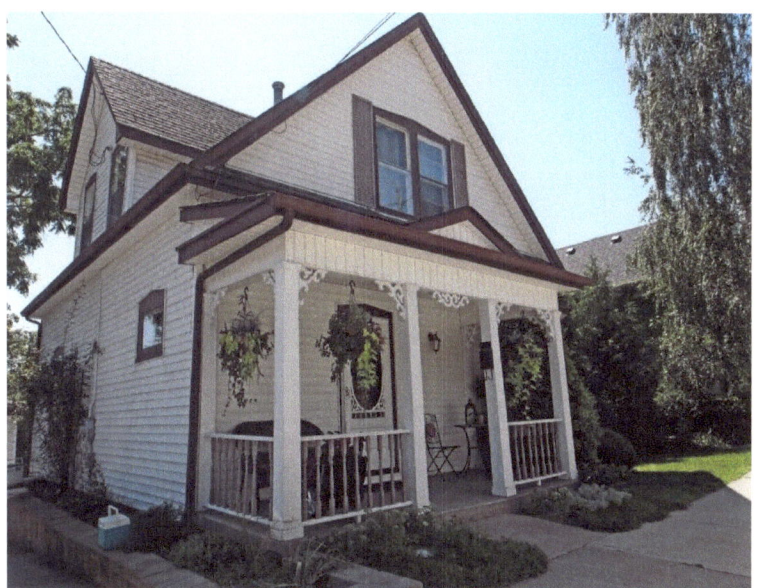

Main Street West - dormer

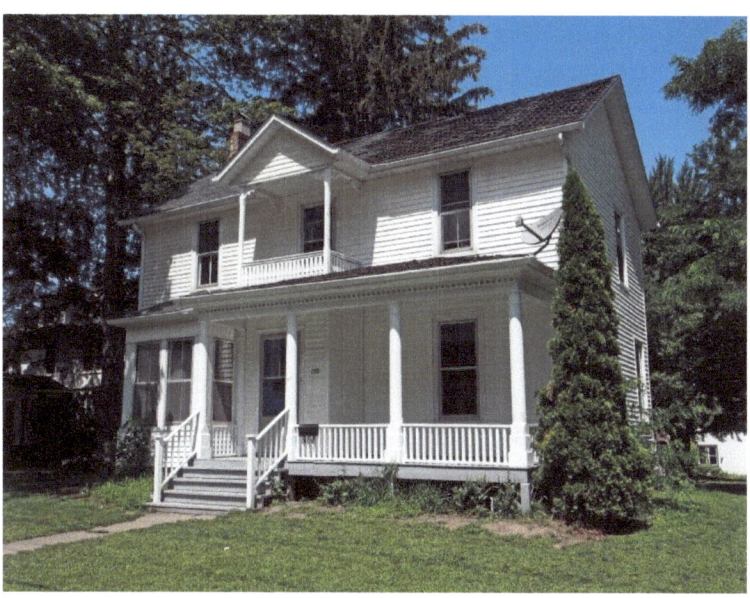

152 Main Street West – second floor balcony with pediment

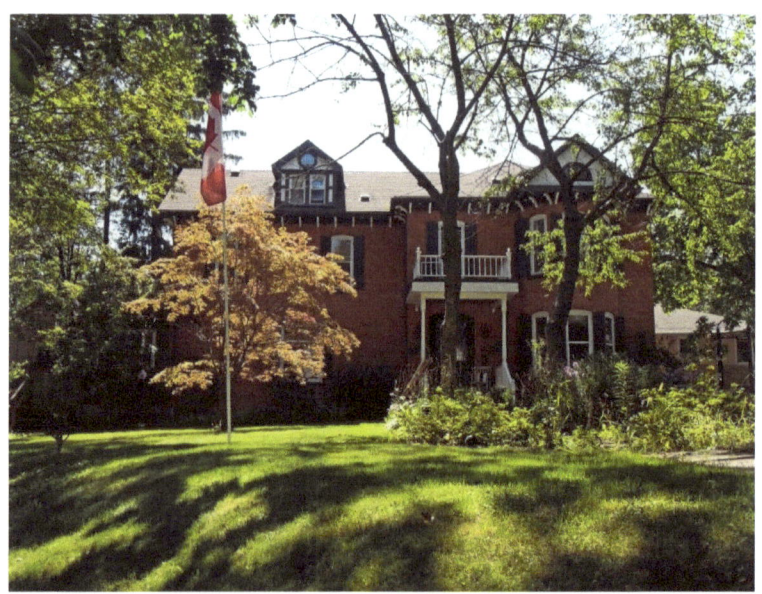

123 Main Street West – Dolmage House – circa 1876 - Robert Dolmage (1820-1889), a general merchant on Main Street, built this red brick home for his wife and daughters. After his wife's death in 1904, the girls care was entrusted to Claude Boden, a shop assistant who had been adopted by Robert. When the last sister Florence died in 1945, she left her estate to Claude who was then free to marry his long-time fiancée Cora March, a teacher at Hagar School.

The historic house now operates as *The Iron Gate Retreat*, a day spa.

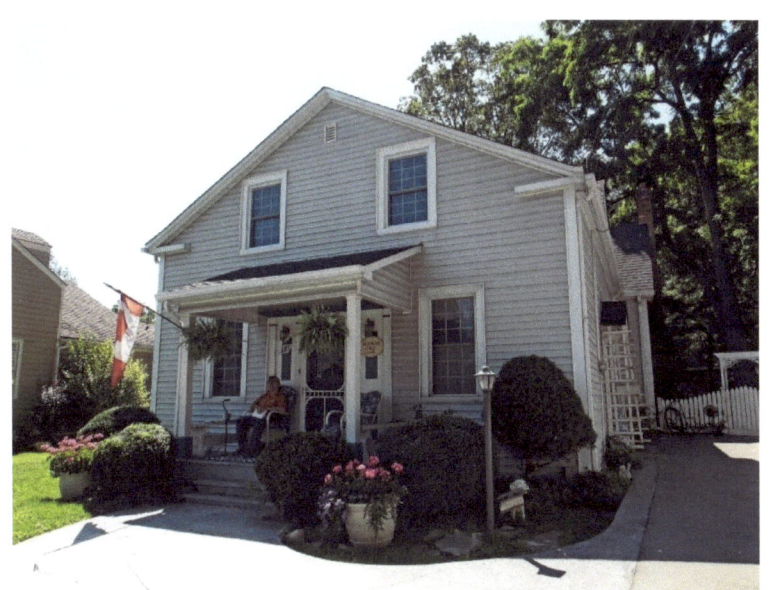

127 Main Street West - This home was originally built as Henry Nelles' merchant shop and granary. The joinery used to build the house indicates that it was originally constructed by ship carpenters. The post and beam interior is made of lovely red pine. At one time this would have been a local gathering place as residents purchased their needed supplies. There is a cornice return on the gable.

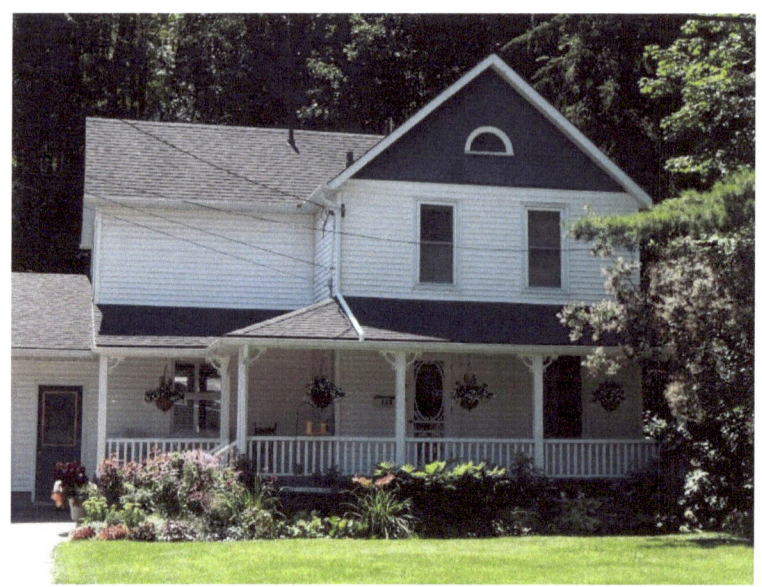

153 Main Street West - half-circle window in gable

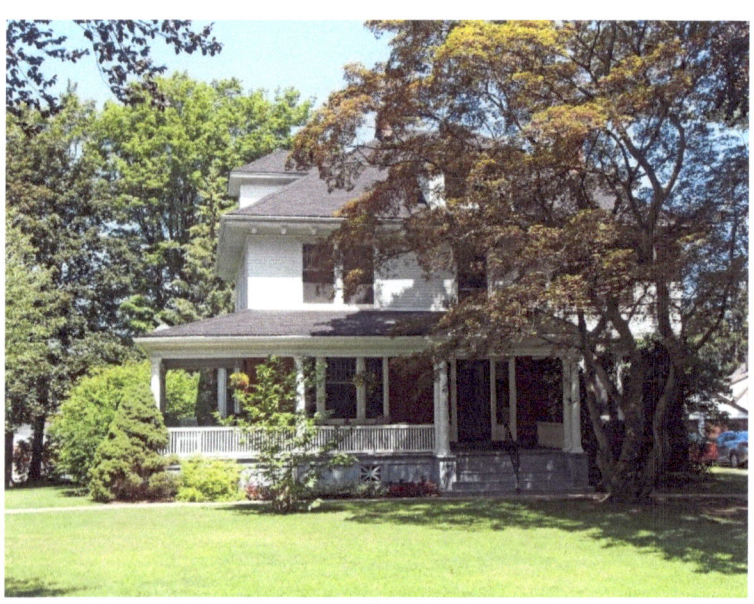

154 Main Street West

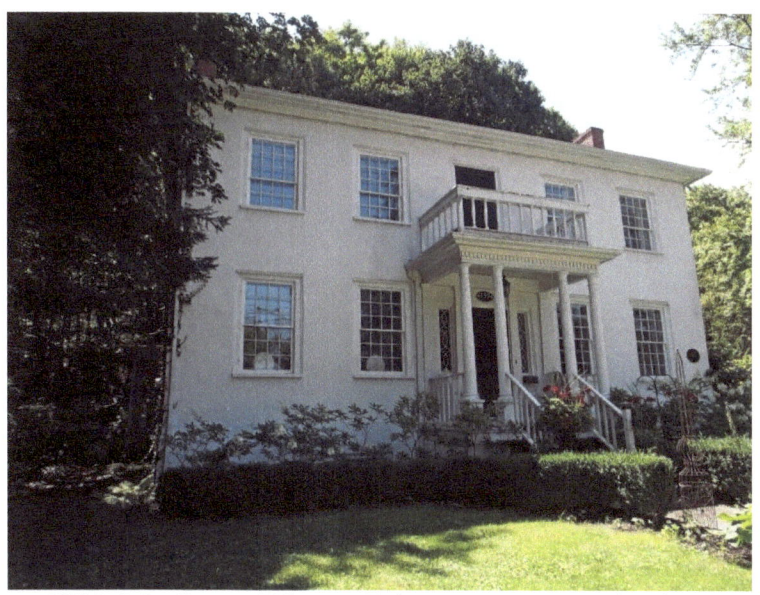

159 Main Street West – White House was built in 1830 by John Grout for his son, Reverend George Grout. The White House is an elegant two-storey Loyalist neo-Classical house in the Georgian style. It is a solid stone house with white plastered walls. The two-tiered porch, a later addition, has four fluted Doric columns with square bases supporting the upper portion of the porch. Plain hand rails are on either side of the main entrance. More decorative balusters and moulded hand rails border the upper tier. A pair of pilasters separates the sidelights from the doorway. The upper windows are in a pattern of twelve panes over eight, the lower larger sash windows are twelve over twelve. The low pitched, hip roof of the main house is trimmed by a plain fascia and moulded soffit. There are three brick chimneys.

The house is said to have served as part of the underground Railroad and a refuge for former slaves.

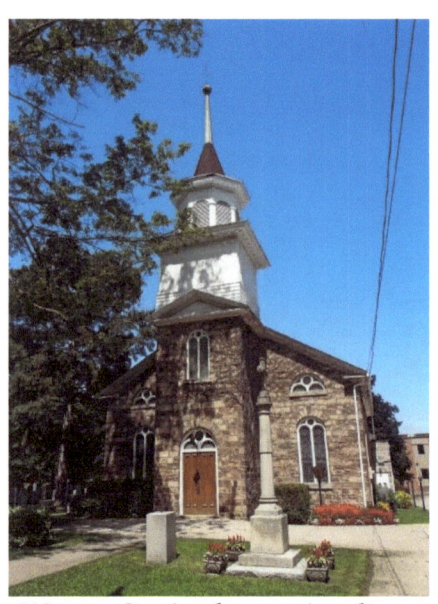

156 Main Street West – St. Andrews Anglican Church – stone church erected 1818-25

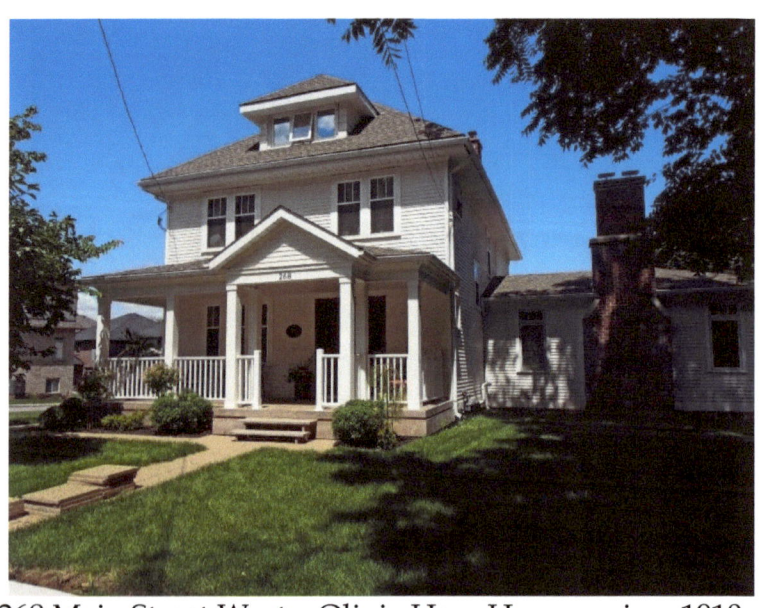

268 Main Street West – Olivia Hare House – circa 1910 – hipped roof with dormer, pediment

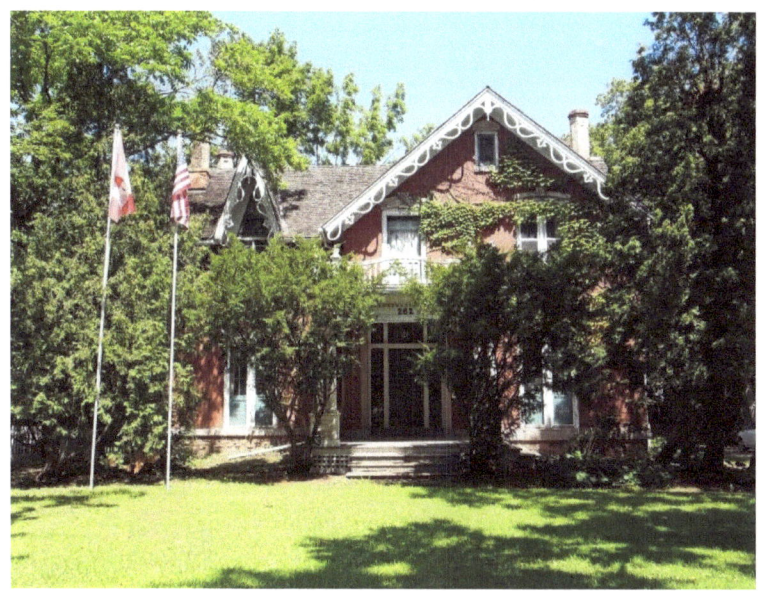

262 Main Street West – Allen Nixon settled on these lands as one of the first United Empire Loyalists in Grimsby. Nixon Hall was built in 1845 as a residence for the Nixon Family. This home demonstrates fine examples of the Gothic elements in its architectural design. The front porch, constructed with classical details, and the north wing are later additions.

The building has a colourful history. It was used as a hostel to house Farmerettes, young women who came from all across Canada to Niagara's *Fruit Belt.* They assisted in farm work and harvest during World War II when many of the young men were away. It was also used as a temporary hospital after the Grimsby hospital burned in 1948. In the one year it was utilized, over 1,000 patients were treated and 288 babies were born in the building.

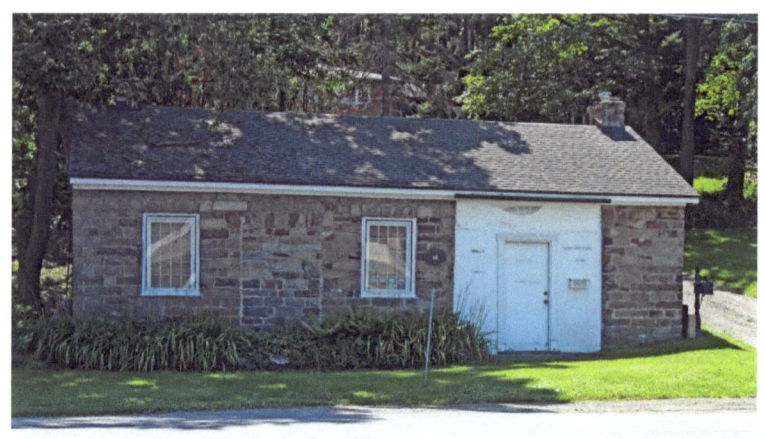

271 Main Street West – Allan Nixon built this little stone blacksmith shop of course rubble around 1800. During the Ware of 1812, British and American forces had their horses shod and equipment repaired here. The building was used as Grimsby's first museum from 1963 to 1983.

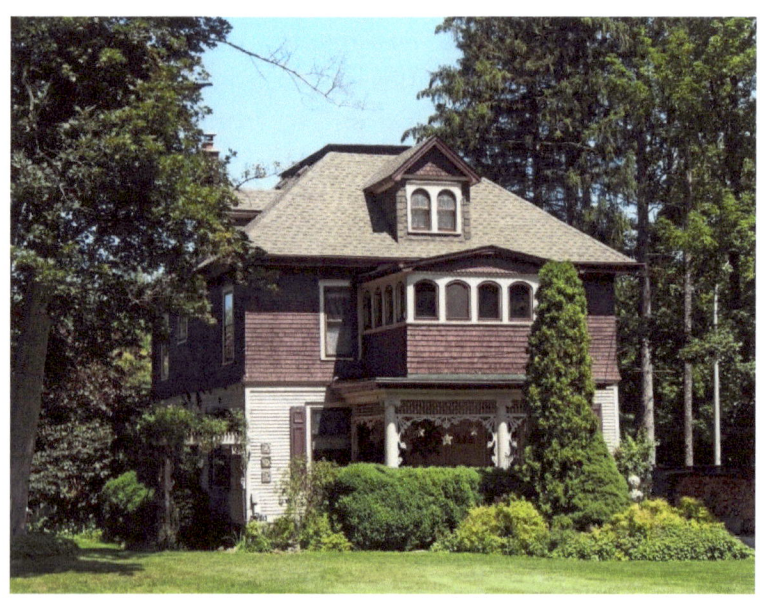

266 Main Street West – dormer, 2nd floor enclosed balcony, bric-a-brac on veranda

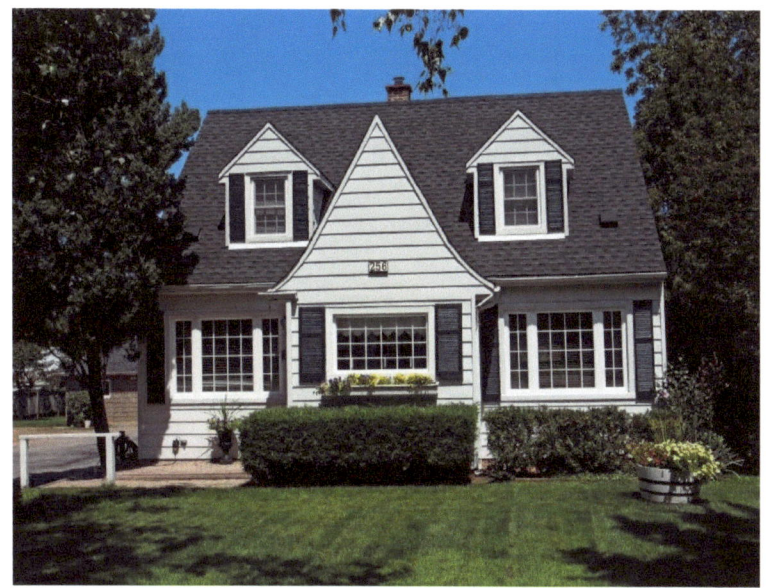

256 Main Street West – Vernacular - dormers

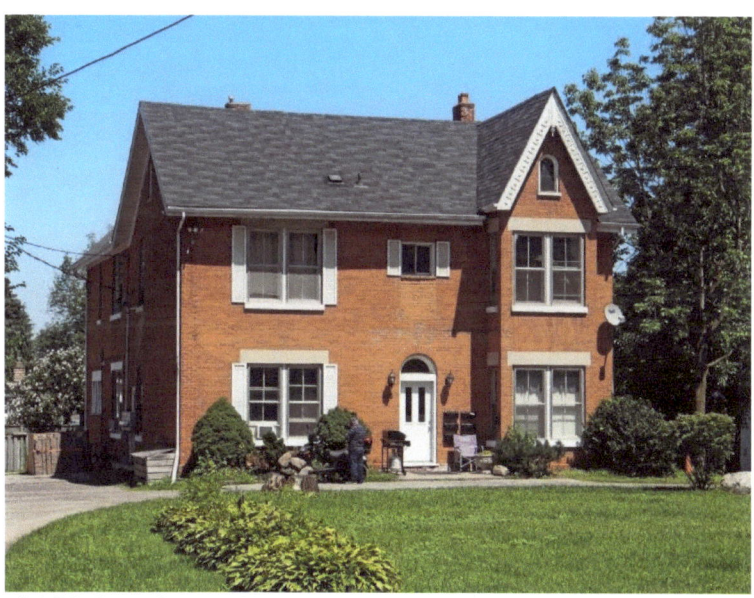

318 Main Street West – transom window above door

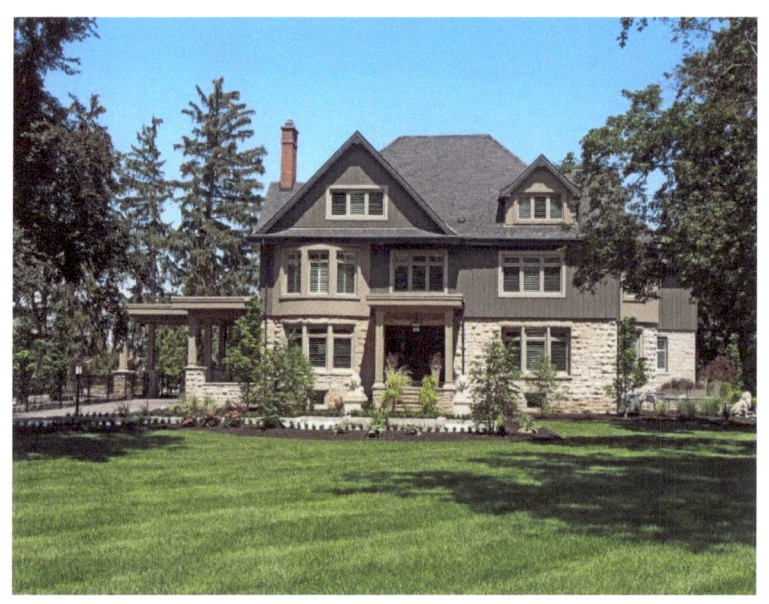

322 Main Street West - stone

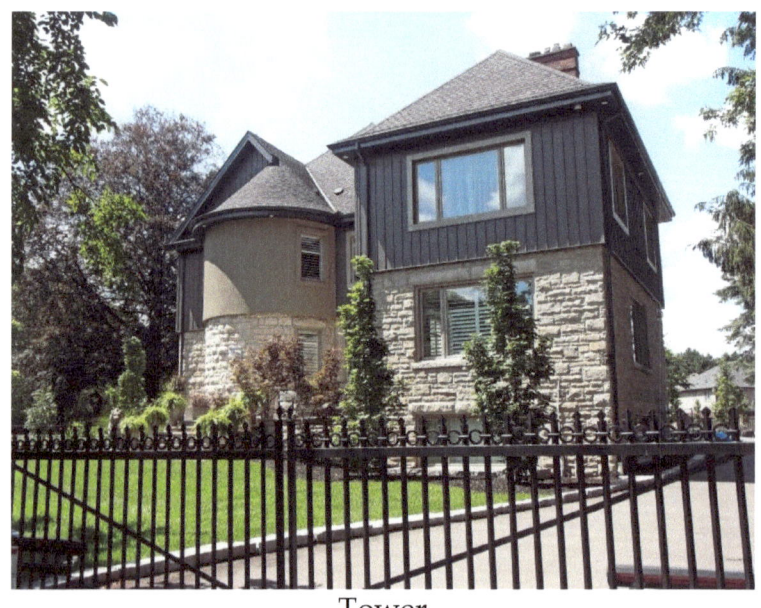

Tower

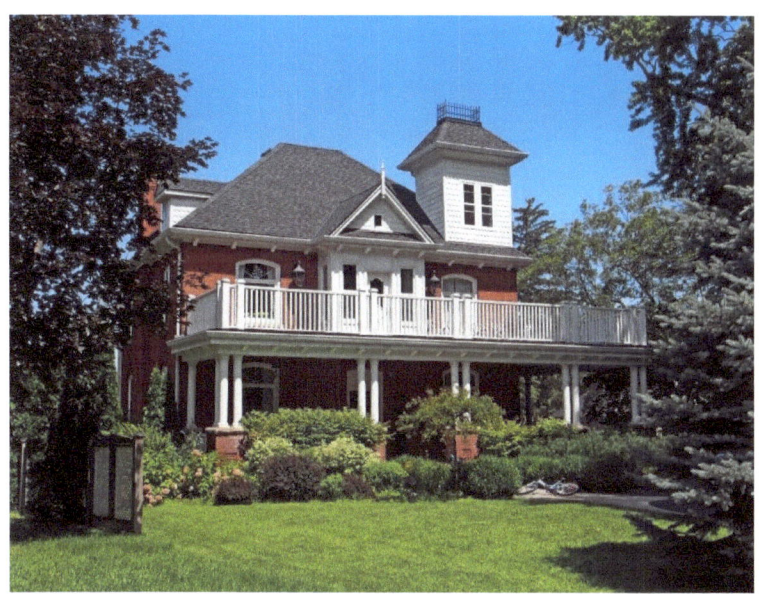

326 Main Street West – turret with widow's walk, full-width 2nd floor balcony

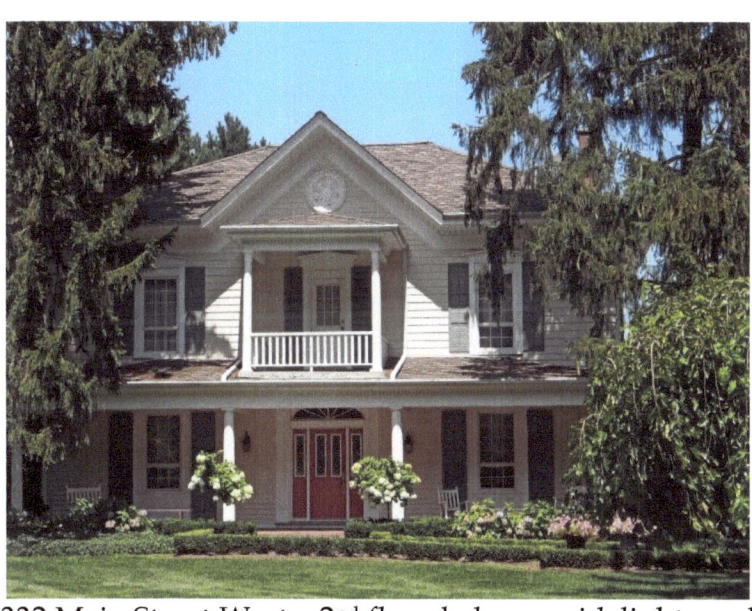

332 Main Street West – 2nd floor balcony, sidelights and transom windows

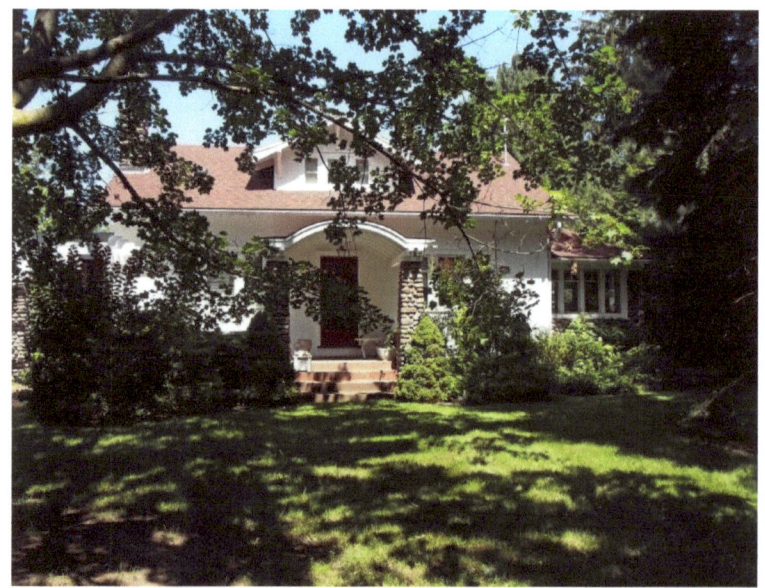

Main Street West – stone porch pillars, dormer in roof

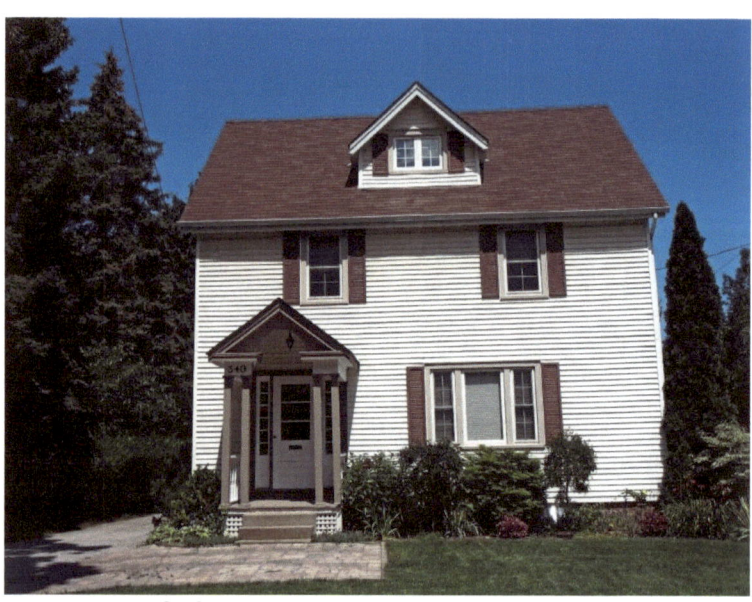

340 Main Street West – dormer,

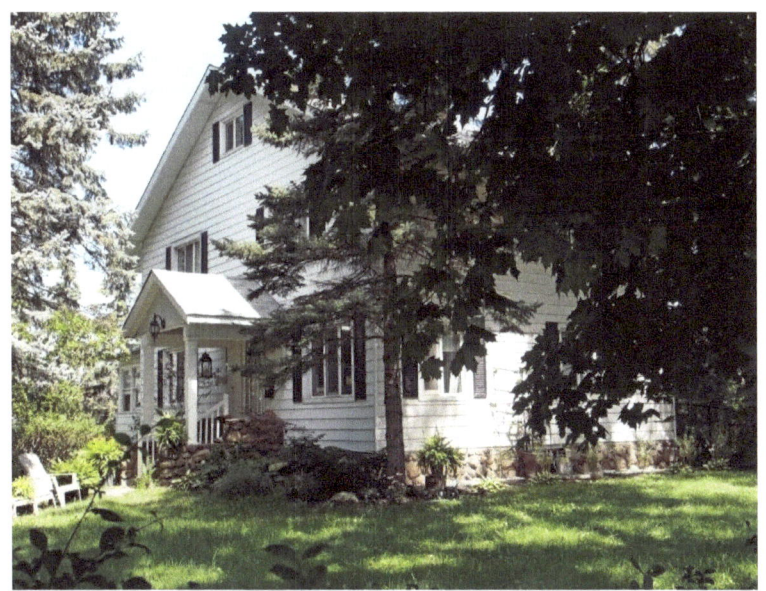

342 Main Street West

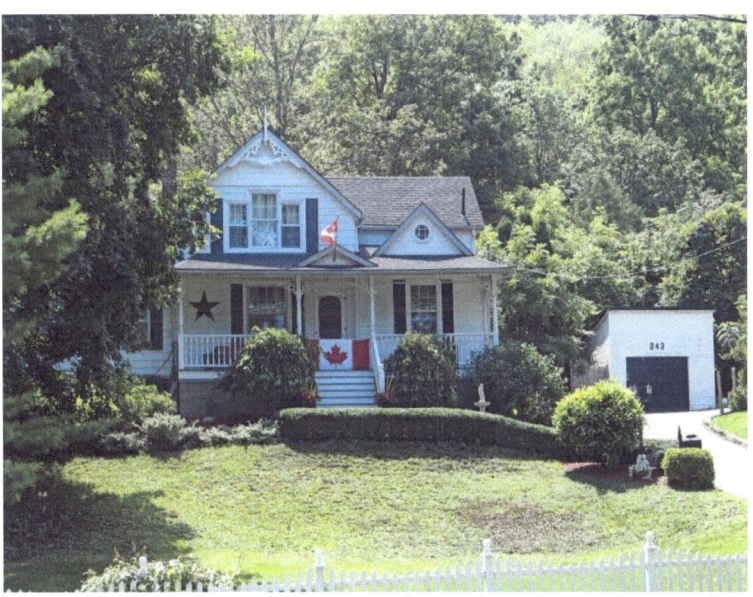

343 Main Street West – verge board and finial on gable

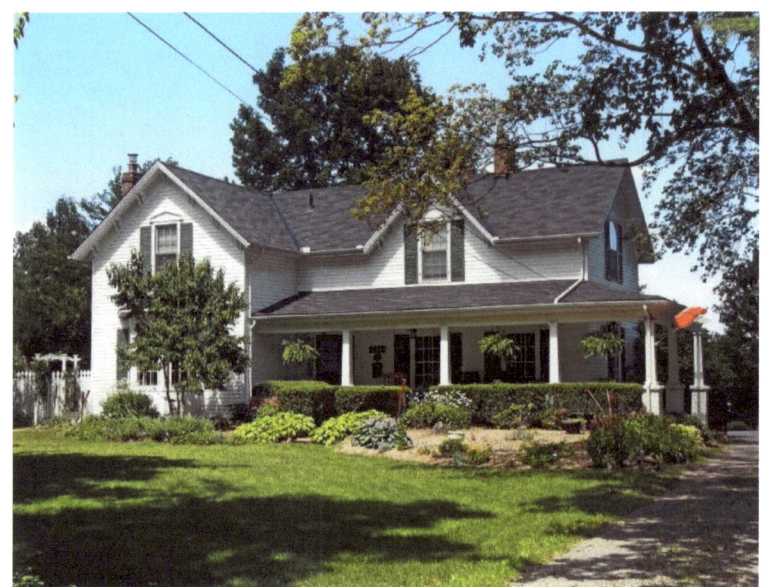

346 Main Street West – C.E. Wolverton House 1840 - Gothic

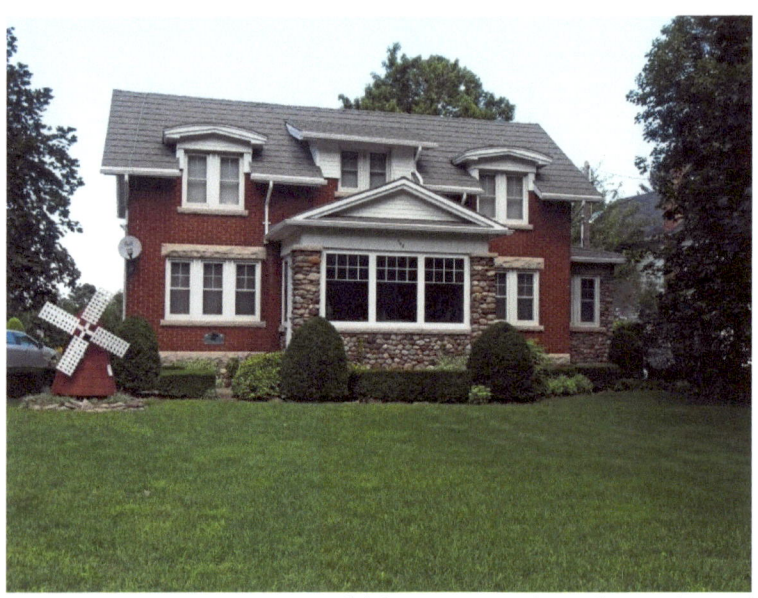

348 Main Street West – cobblestone enclosed porch with pediment, dormers in attic

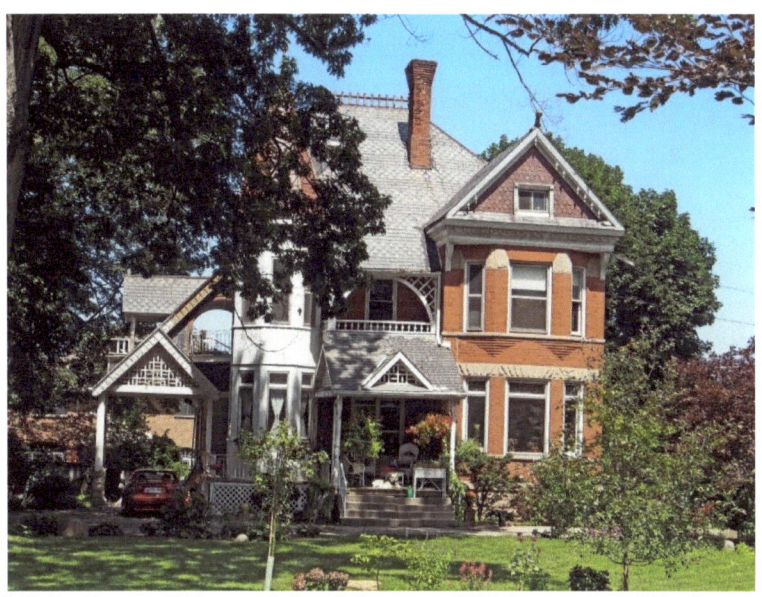

354 Main Street West – Maplehurst - With a mix of Italianate, Queen Anne and Romanesque Revival styles, this beautiful Victorian home has everything – two-storey bay windows, gables, porches, a veranda, and even a tower. It was built circa 1880 by Linus Wolverton a fruit farmer since 1798. In addition to growing fruit, Linus was editor of The Canadian Horticulturist, secretary of the Ontario Fruit Growers Association, and Inspector of Experimental Stations. Maplehurst was one of these stations.

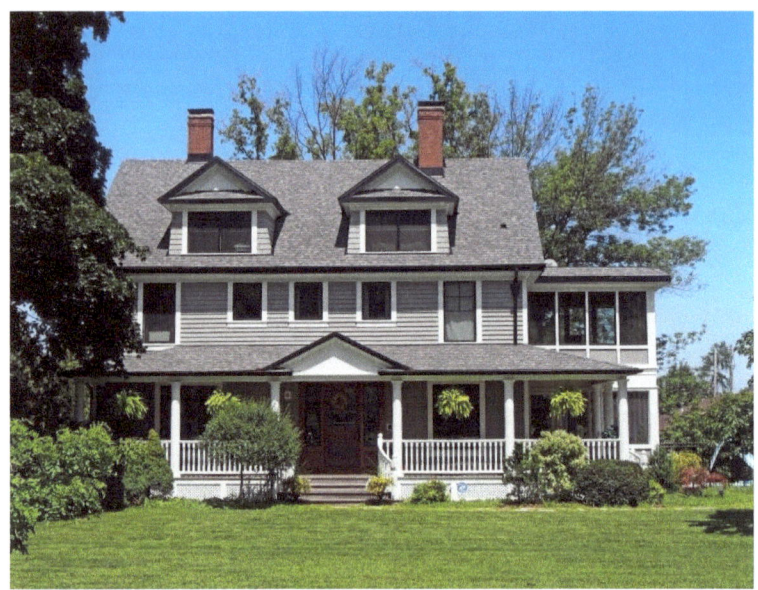

360 Main Street West - dormers

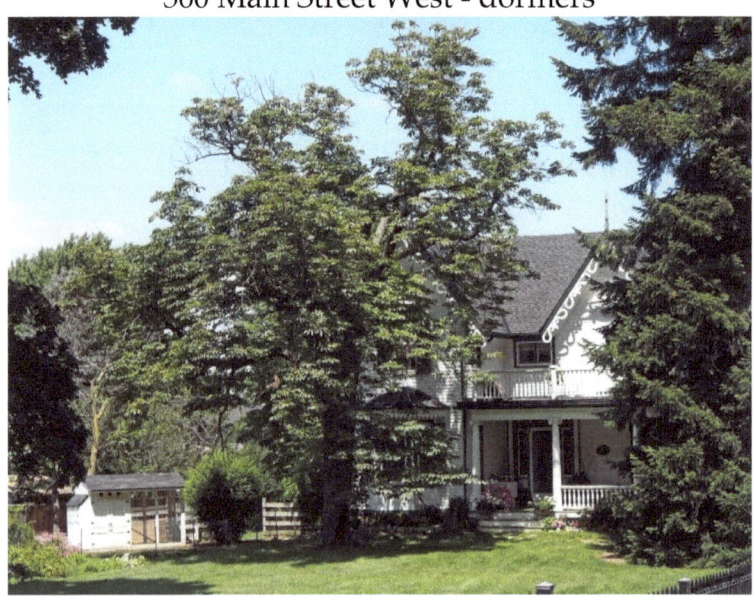

366 Main Street West – Gothic – verge board on gables – Echo Hall was built in 1842 by C. Woolverton. There is a panelled front door, bow-tie barge board around the eaves and a large veranda.

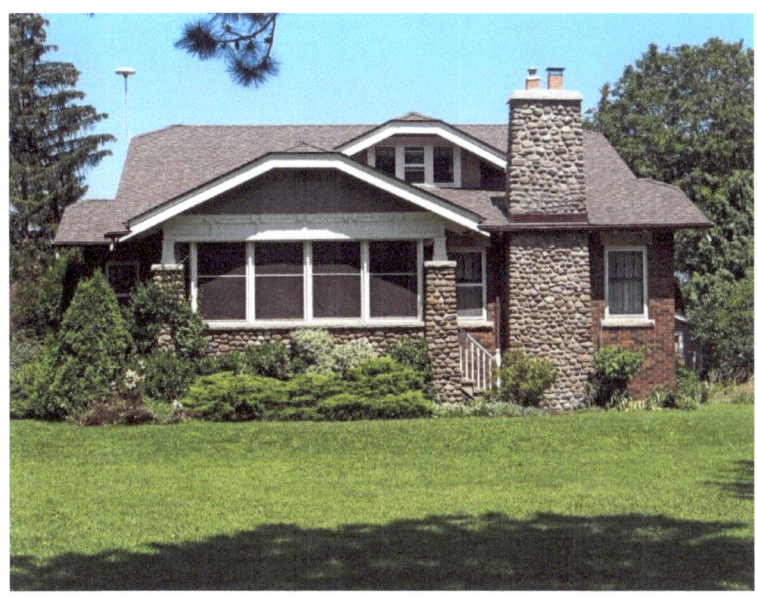

386 Main Street West – chipped gables with matching dormer; cobblestone chimney, porch pillars and wall

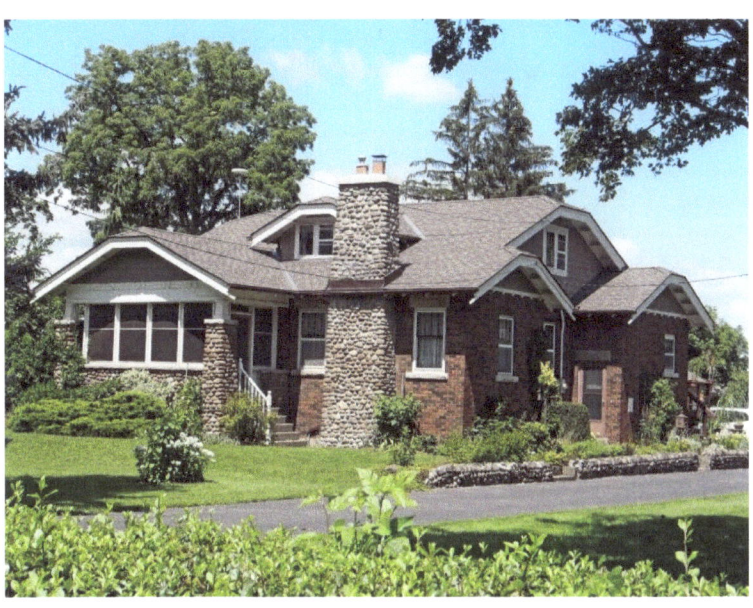

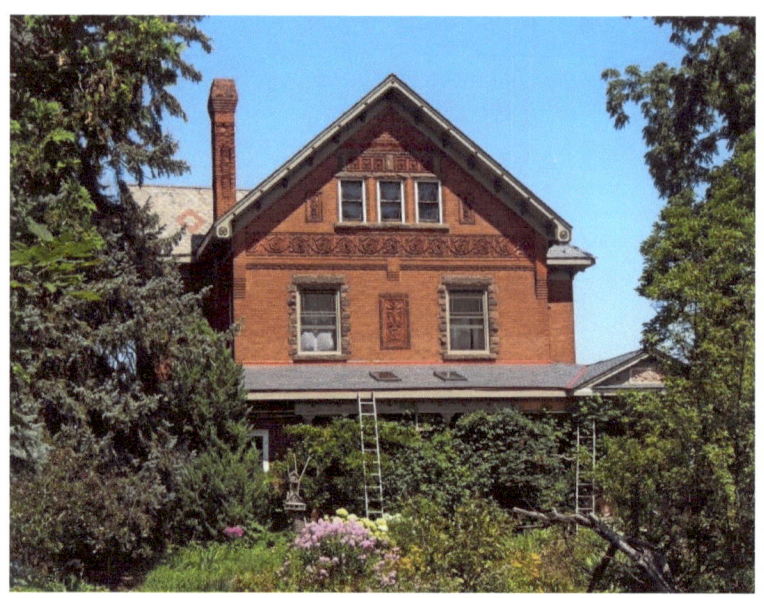

378 Main Street West – terra cotta trim

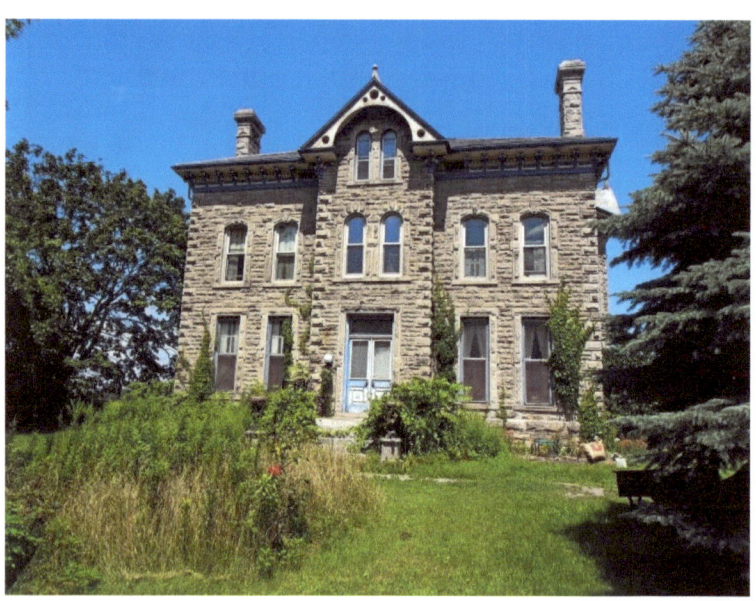

390 Main Street West

390 Main Street West – names for the house are Smith-Geddes House, Thornfield Hall, The Stone House - The two-and-a-half-storey stone building was constructed between 1876 and 1878. The Smith-Geddes House was built on a flat area of land amidst orchards of peach and cherry trees. The rural location, close to Lake Ontario to the northeast and the Niagara escarpment to the southwest, creates a unique natural setting.

Born in 1828, John Henry Smith was a descendent of one of the area's earliest settlers, United Empire Loyalist John Smith. John Smith came with his wife and children to the Grimsby area in 1787, and settled on a land grant between the Niagara escarpment and Lake Ontario. Smith-Geddes House was built for his son, John Henry Smith, a businessman and entrepreneur.

Known as John Henry 'California' Smith because of the fortune he made in the California Gold Rush, in 1849, John Henry Smith later founded a successful gold mine in Colorado. Upon his return to Grimsby, John Henry had his house built on land that was originally part of his grandfather's estate. It is an important example of a high-Victorian country house in the Italianate architectural style rendered in a vernacular form. John Henry and his wife lived in the house for over thirty years until their deaths. The house remained in the family and came into the possession of the Geddes family, relatives of the Smiths. Dora Geddes was a great-great granddaughter of Loyalist settler John Smith and she lived in the house for over thirty years until her death. The house was bought by the Germann family, who retained ownership for over forty years, subdividing the house into apartments. The house is once again a single family home.

The stone house has a five bay façade with a projecting frontispiece, containing the main entrance of wood paneled doors, a transom of colored glass and the etched initials of John Henry Smith. Paired round-headed windows above the centre door and a smaller pair on the third floor are under a projecting gable, with a carved-wood verge board. The hip, patterned-slate roof has corniced edges of wood brackets, supporting the soffit. Four chimneys of quarry-faced stone, laid in random ashlar, project from each corner of the house and are decorated with pediment moldings along the stacks. The two flanking bays of the main façade have pairs of square-headed windows on the first floor and segmented arches on the second. The stone work is quarry-faced ashlar with projecting rusticated quoins and window surrounds. A projecting wing on the west side is capped with a gable. A wide bay window with a gable roof projects from the east side.

The interior is laid out in a centre-hall plan with an ornate wood staircase. The interior woodwork is walnut and oak, with carved mantels in both the east parlor and the dining room. The hallway and stairs are paneled in cherry. The wood windows have louvered shutters that fold into reveals matching the paneling of the windows and detailed baseboards are found throughout. The hall, east parlor and dining room have plaster moldings and plaster ceiling medallions. Elaborate cast-iron grills surround the radiators in each of the rooms. The original porch has been removed and a number of small additions have been made to the rear of the house, including a fire escape.

Architectural Terms

Battlement: A design for a parapet that has alternating solid parts and openings, originally used for defense, but later used as a decorative motif. Example: 22 Main Street West, Page 27	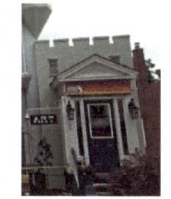
Bay Window: A window that projects out from a wall, in a semicircular, rectangular, or polygonal design. Used frequently in Gothic and Victorian designs. Example: 99 Main Street West, Page 39	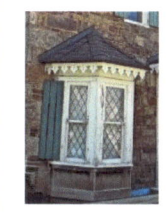
Brackets: a decorative or weight-bearing structural element which forms a right angle with one side against a wall and the other under a projecting surface such as an eave or roof. Example: 43 Main Street East, Page 22	
Capital: The uppermost finish or decoration on a column. An Ionic column has a small base, a thin elegant shaft, and a capital composed of volutes which are carved whirls or twists that take the form of a scroll. Example: 96 Main Street East, Page 18 A Doric column is characterized by a plain column with no base, a shaft with twenty flutings, and a simple capital with a simple entablature. Example: 84 Main Street East, Page 20	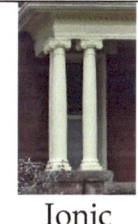 Ionic 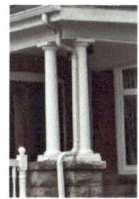 Doric

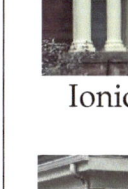

Dentil Moulding: an even series of rectangles used as ornamental decoration in cornices. Example: 47 Main Street West, Page 31	
Dichromatic brickwork: the use of two colours of brick, tile or slate to decorate a façade. Example: 91 Main Street East, Page 19	
Dormer: (French for "sleep") a gable end window that pierces through the plane of a sloping roof surface to create usable space in the top floor or attic of a building by adding headroom. Example: 239 Main Street East, Page 7	
Fretwork: interlaced decorative design resembling a bracket Example: Main Street East, Page 20	
Frontispiece: a portion of the façade of a building, usually a centred doorway that is slightly raised from the rest of the building, usually has extensive ornamentation. Frontispieces are usually Classical in design with white columned porches. Example: 390 Main Street West, Page 58	
Gable: the triangular portion of a wall between the edges of a sloping roof. Example: 92 Main Street West, Page 38	

Gambrel Roof: a symmetrical two-sided roof with two slopes on each side; the upper slope is positioned at a shallow angle, while the lower slope is steep. It is similar to a mansard roof, but a gambrel has vertical gable ends instead of being hipped at the four corners of the building. Example: 66 Main Street East, Page 21	
Hipped Roof: a roof where all sides slope downwards to the walls with no gables. Example: 78 Main Street East, Page 20	
Keystones and Voussoirs: a voussoir is a wedge-shaped element used in building an arch. A keystone is the central stone that locks all the stones into position, allowing the arch to bear weight. A keystone is often enlarged and embellished. Example: 43 Main Street East, Page 22	
Palladian Window: a large window that is divided into three sections with the centre section larger than the two side sections and usually arched. Example: 84 Main Street East, Page 20	
Parapet: low wall around the edge of a roof. Example: 35 Main Street West, Page 29	
Pediment: a triangular section above the door or portico, usually supported by columns. The inside of the triangle is called the tympanum. Example: 92 Main Street East, Page 18	

Quoin: masonry blocks at the corner of a wall, often a decorative feature, usually larger or of a different colour than the rest of the wall. Example: 91 Main Street East, Page 19	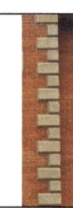
Sidelight: a vertical window that flanks a door, and is often used to emphasize the importance of a primary entrance. **Transom Window:** the light above the doorway, also called a fanlight. Example: 332 Main Street West, Page 50	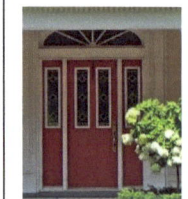
Tower: A circular, square, or octagonal vertical structure higher than the surrounding structure that is usually part of an existing building and is created either for extra defense or for a specific purpose such as a clock or a bell tower. Example: 22 Main Street West, Page 27	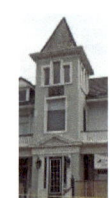
Turret: a small tower that projects from the wall of a building. Example: 22 Main Street West, Page 27	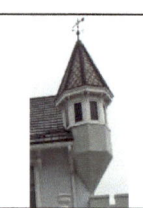
Verge board and Finial: also called bargeboards – hang from the projecting end of a roof and are often elaborately carved and ornamented. **Finial:** ornament added to the top of a gable, pinnacle, canopy or spire – a Gothic element. Example: 343 Main Street West, Page 62	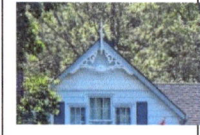

Building Styles

Georgian, before 1860 – This style began with the British King Georges in the 18th century. These buildings have balanced facades around a central door, medium-pitched gable roofs, and small paned windows. Example: 126 Main Street West, Page 32	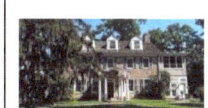
Gothic Revival, 1830-1890 – These decorative buildings have sharply-pitched gables with highly detailed verge boards, pointed-arch window openings, and dichromatic brickwork. It is a common style in Ontario. Example: 346 Main Street West, Page 53	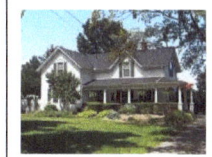
Italianate, 1850-1900 – A two story rectangular building with a mild hip roof, a projecting frontispiece, and generous eaves with ornate cornice brackets was the basis of the style; often there are large sash windows, quoins, ornate detailing on the windows, belvederes and wraparound verandahs. Italianate commercial buildings often have cast iron cresting and elegant window surrounds. Example: 390 Main Street West, Page 58	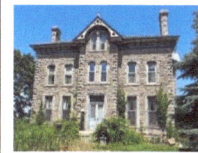

Neo-colonial (also Colonial Revival, Georgian Revival or Neo-Georgian) architecture seeks to revive elements of architectural style of American colonial architecture of the period around the Revolutionary War which drew strongly from Georgian architecture of Great Britain. It includes a wide assortment of detailing and ornament applied to a design centered around the fireplace and the source of water. Structures are typically two stories, have a symmetrical front facade with elaborate front doorways, often with decorative crown pediments, fanlights, and sidelights, symmetrical windows flanking the front entrance, often in pairs or threes, and columned porches. Example: 66 Main Street East, Page 22	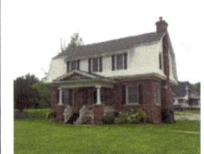
Regency Cottage, 1830-1860 – This style originated in England in 1815 and spread to Ontario later in the 19th century as British officers retired to Canada. It is a modest one-storey house with a low-pitched hip roof and has a symmetrical front façade. Example: 129 Main Street West, Page 35	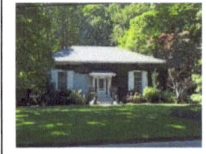

Vernacular/Traditional Mode 1638 - 1950 Influenced but not defined by a particular style, vernacular buildings are made from easily available materials and exhibit local design characteristics. Example: 256 Main Street West, Page 49	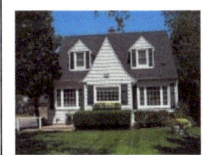
Victorian - In Ontario, a Victorian style building can be seen as any building built between 1840 and 1900 that doesn't fit into any of the other categories. It encompasses a large group of buildings constructed in brick, stone, and timber, using an eclectic mixture of Classical and Gothic motifs. Example: 354 Main Street West, Page 55	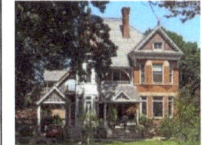

www.ingramcontent.com/pod-product-compliance
Lightning Source LLC
Chambersburg PA
CBHW040234220526
45473CB00001B/234